DRAMA CLASSICS

The Drama Classics series aims to offer the world's greatest plays in affordable paperback editions for students, actors and theatregoers. The hallmarks of the series are accessible introductions, uncluttered and uncut texts and an overall theatrical perspective.

Given that readers may be encountering a particular play for the first time, the introduction seeks to fill in the theatrical/ historical background and to outline the chief themes rather than concentrate on interpretational and textual analysis. Similarly the play-texts themselves are free of footnotes and other interpolations: instead there is an end-glossary of 'difficult' words and phrases.

The texts of the English-language plays in the series have been prepared taking full account of all existing scholarship. The foreign language plays have been newly translated into a modern English that is both actable and accurate: many of the translators regularly have their work staged professionally.

Under the editorship of Kenneth McLeish, the Drama Classics series is building into a first-class library of dramatic literature representing the best of world theatre.

Series editor: Kenneth McLeish

Associate editors:

Professor Trevor R. Griffiths, *School of Literary and Media Studies, University of North London*

Simon Trussler, *Reader in Drama, Goldsmiths' College, University of London*

DRAMA CLASSICS *the first hundred*

The Alchemist
All for Love
Amphitryon
Andromache
Antigone
Arden of Faversham
Bacchae
The Beaux Stratagem
The Beggar's Opera
Birds
Blood Wedding
Brand
The Broken Jug
The Changeling
The Cherry Orchard
Children of the Sun
El Cid
The Country Wife
Cyrano de Bergerac
The Dance of Death
The Devil is an Ass
Doctor Faustus
A Doll's House
Don Juan
The Duchess of Malfi
Edward II
Electra (Euripides)
Electra (Sophocles)
An Enemy of the
    People
Enrico IV
The Eunuch
Every Man in his
    Humour
Everyman
The Father
Faust
A Flea in her Ear
Frogs
Fuenteovejuna

The Game of Love
    and Chance
Ghosts
The Government
    Inspector
Hedda Gabler
The Hypochondriac
The Importance of
    Being Earnest
An Italian Straw Hat
The Jew of Malta
King Oedipus
The Learned Ladies
Life is a Dream
The Lower Depths
The Lucky Chance
Lulu
Lysistrata
The Magistrate
The Malcontent
The Man of Mode
The Marriage of Figaro
Mary Stuart
The Master Builder
Medea
Menaechmi
The Misanthrope
The Miser
Miss Julie
Molière
A Month in the
    Country
A New Way to Pay
    Old Debts
Oedipus at Kolonos
The Oresteia
Phaedra
Philoctetes
The Playboy of the
    Western World

The Revenger's
    Tragedy
The Rivals
The Robbers
La Ronde
The Rover
The School for
    Scandal
The Seagull
The Servant of Two
    Masters
She Stoops to
    Conquer
The Shoemaker's
    Holiday
Six Characters in
    Search of an
    Author
Spring's Awakening
Strife
Tartuffe
Thérèse Raquin
Three Sisters
'Tis Pity she's a
    Whore
Too Clever by Half
Ubu
Uncle Vanya
Volpone
The Way of the World
The White Devil
The Wild Duck
Women Beware
    Women
Women of Troy
Woyzeck
Yerma

*The publishers welcome
suggestions for further titles*

T243

DRAMA CLASSICS

THE GOVERNMENT INSPECTOR

by
Nikolai Gogol

translated and with an introduction by
Stephen Mulrine

NICK HERN BOOKS
London

A Drama Classic

The Government Inspector first published in Great Britain
in this translation as a paperback original in 1997
by Nick Hern Books Limited, 14 Larden Road, London W3 7ST.

Reprinted 1999

Copyright in the translation from the Russian © 1997
by Stephen Mulrine

Copyright in the introduction © 1997 Nick Hern Books Limited

Stephen Mulrine has asserted his moral right to be identified
as the translator of this work.

Typeset by Country Setting, Woodchurch, Kent TN26 3TB
Printed by Watkiss Studios Limited, Biggleswade, Beds SG18 9ST

A CIP catalogue record for this book is available from the
British Library

ISBN 1 85459 174 6

Introduction

Nikolai Vasilievich Gogol (1809 – 1852)

Gogol was born on March 20th, 1809, at Sorochintsy in the Ukraine. Gogol's family belonged to the minor Russian-speaking nobility, and his father had some literary pretensions, writing plays based on Ukrainian folk-tales. The young Gogol is said to have shown considerable acting talent at the local high school, from which he graduated in 1828, at the age of nineteen. Intent on a career in the government service, Gogol moved to St. Petersburg, but failed to find employment, either as a civil servant or as an actor.

In July 1829, he attempted to launch a literary career with a sentimental idyll, *Hans Küchelgarten*, published under a pseudonym, but the work attracted such unfavourable reviews that Gogol bought up all the unsold copies and made a bonfire of them, before leaving for Germany, where he remained until September. On his return to Russia, Gogol's fortunes took a turn for the better, and in 1831 he succeeded in obtaining a post as a teacher of history in a young women's college.

In September of that year, Gogol published a collection of tales of Ukrainian village life, *Evenings on a Farm near Dikanka*, which met with immediate critical acclaim, including that of the great Pushkin himself, and with the appearance of a second volume, in March 1832, Gogol was established as an important new voice.

A career in education still beckoned, however, and although he began work on a comedy, *Vladimir Third Class*, his pedagogic ambitions were perhaps over-fulfilled with his appointment as assistant professor of history at the University of St Petersburg in July 1834. At any rate, Gogol continued to write, and the following year saw the publication of *Arabesques*, essays and stories of life in the capital, including *Nevsky Prospect*, *The Portrait*, and the extraordinary *Diary of a Madman*, in addition to another collection centred on his native Ukraine, *Mirgorod*.

Gogol soon tired of academic life, and his departure from the university in December was crowned by the completion of *The Government Inspector*, which was given its first performance on April 19th, 1836, at the Aleksandrinsky Theatre in St Petersburg. The play was an instant hit, but Gogol became alarmed at attempts by both left and right-wing critics to turn it into a *cause célèbre*, and again left the country, settling eventually in Rome, where he remained for the next eleven years, returning to his homeland only twice, to oversee publication of his books.

In 1843, a four-volume collection of his works appeared, which consolidated his fame, and it was during these years of voluntary exile that Gogol's prose masterpieces were completed: *Taras Bulba*, *Dead Souls*, and perhaps his most influential short story, *The Overcoat*, which would later prompt Dostoevsky to observe: 'We have all emerged from under Gogol's overcoat.'

Gogol himself, however, continued to agonize, morally and spiritually, over the purpose of his fiction, and in the summer of 1845 he burned the manuscript of the second volume of *Dead Souls*, destroying five years' work. And the following year, the erstwhile hero of the liberals published his notorious *Selected Passages from Correspondence with Friends*, a reactionary defence of the Tsarist autocracy and serfdom. Again, Gogol was taken aback by the hostility it encountered, including a ferocious diatribe from the radical critic Belinsky, his former champion, and in 1848 he embarked on a pilgrimage to the Holy Land, in a vain search for spiritual solace.

In his latter years, after his return to Russia in 1848, Gogol fell prey to religious mania, aggravated by the influence of a fanatical Orthodox priest, Father Matvei, and became chronically ill through dangerous ascetic practices. Towards the end of his life, Gogol was so emaciated that his vertebrae could be felt through his stomach. On February 11th, 1852, in a final act of creative self-immolation, he burned the rewritten second volume of *Dead Souls*, and died ten days later, from exhaustion and malnutrition, at the age of forty-two.

The Government Inspector: **What Happens in the Play**

In all essentials, Gogol's 'case of mistaken identity' is a comic warhorse of some pedigree, reaching back to classical times and forward to our own day in seemingly inexhaustible variation. A penniless stranger arrives in a small provincial town, is mistaken for a VIP, treated like royalty by all and sundry, and eventually exposed – making his hosts look extremely foolish. Gogol's variation, on his own evidence, came from Pushkin, in response to a letter he sent to the great poet, seeking a subject for a comedy. Pushkin obliged with an anecdote from his own experience, having himself been mistaken for an important government official, on a trip to the Volga region a few years previously. However, Gogol was also influenced by Corneille and Molière, and perhaps by a Russian comedy on a similar theme by Kvitka, written in 1827, and titled *A Visitor From the Capital*.

Detail is all-important in Gogol's work, and *The Government Inspector* is no exception. Almost the whole of Act One, for example, is devoted to painting a picture of his nameless provincial mudhole, and its corrupt and self-serving administrators, long before the play's eponymous 'hero' makes his entrance, in the squalid inn which is the setting for Act Two.

Khlestakov, the bogus inspector, is in fact a low-grade civil servant, travelling from St Petersburg to his family home – a young man living beyond his means, a follower of fashion, and inveterate card-player, temporarily h led up at the local inn, and unable to pay his bill. However, while Khlestakov and his manservant Osip debate where their next meal is to come from, the town mayor is at that moment reading out the contents of a letter to an urgently convened assembly of local officials and dignitaries.

The letter warns of an impending visit by a government inspector, travelling incognito, and the anxious officials attempt to plan a strategy for keeping their various swindles under wraps, at least for the duration of the visit. The mayor himself might be described as bribe-taker in chief, preying on the local traders; the judge, obsessed with riding to hounds, treats his court as an extension of his tack-room; the postmaster diligently unseals the mail, and retails its contents as gossip; the charities warden, and a compliant workhouse physician maintain their charges on a régime of strict discipline and no expensive medicaments. Embezzlement is routine, the town is run for private profit, and the officials are further panicked when two local landowners, Bobchinsky and Dobchinsky, burst in to announce that the government inspector, in the person of Khlestakov, is in their very midst!

The mayor promptly leads a delegation to Khlestakov's inn, settles the latter's unpaid account, and arranges for his removal to more comfortable quarters, i.e., his own mansion, where Khlestakov, the sophisticated St Petersburg dandy, instantly becomes a focus for the amorous yearnings not only of the mayor's daughter, but also of his wife. While Khlestakov is enjoying life at the mayor's house, he receives a series of visits from the guilt-ridden officials, each more eager than the last to purchase his favour, with extravagant 'loans'.

Word of the inspector's presence has filtered down to the long-suffering citizenry, however, and a deputation of traders and artisans also arrives with a catalogue of grievances for Khlestakov, accusing the mayor. Siberian exile, at the very least, appears to beckon, but in a neat twist, Khlestakov is inveigled into proposing marriage to the mayor's daughter. Overcome with relief, now that his position is secure, the mayor envisages a glittering career in St Petersburg. Khlestakov, meanwhile, has yielded to the urgings of his manservant Osip to quit while ahead, and is already miles away by the time the post-master unseals his letter to a St Petersburg journalist crony, revealing all.

Finally, just as it seems the nadir has been reached, with the townsfolk's realisation that they have been willing dupes, a policeman enters with the news that a genuine government inspector has arrived, and is waiting for them at the inn. The mayor and his officials, his wife and daughter, their various guests, all freeze in a dumb show precisely described by Gogol, a literal monument to human greed and folly.

The Government Inspector

Gogol began writing *The Government Inspector* in the autumn of 1835, and the fact that it received its first performance a mere six months later is itself worthy of note, given the rigours of the Tsarist censorship. (Pushkin, for example, died without ever seeing *Boris Godunov* performed, and Ostrovsky waited nine years for the first public staging of his satire *A Family Affair*, with a rewritten 'moral' ending, moreover, supplied by the censor.) By good fortune, however, Gogol showed his latest creation to the poet Zhukovsky, who was also tutor to the young Crown Prince, and the play thus came under the Tsar's personal scrutiny. In a magnanimous gesture of the kind he occasionally permitted himself, Nicholas ordered *The Government Inspector* to be performed at the Aleksandrinsky Imperial Theatre in St Petersburg, and the première duly took place on April 19th, 1836. The Tsar himself was in the audience, expressed his delight, and added: 'Everyone has received his due, myself most of all.'

Gogol's brilliant comedy, however, attracted praise and condemnation in equal measure: to the radical intelligentsia, it was a welcome indictment of the corrupt and inefficient Tsarist regime; to the conservatives, it was unpatriotic and subversive. Not for the last time, Gogol was driven to explain his intention, and in a letter to Zhukovsky, he expressed his annoyance that both wings of Russian opinion appeared to see the play as offering a challenge to the established order, whereas his satire was directed only at individuals who took the law into their own hands, in defiance of that order.

In this respect, it is significant that the play's action, as distinct from its final tableau, concludes with the off-stage arrival of the genuine inspector, who will presumably call the miscreants to heel and re-establish good government. No doubt if Gogol had followed Molière's example in *Le Tartuffe*, and furnished his audience with a lengthy disclaimer, he might have spared himself some heartache, but while the play benefits immensely from its steel-trap ending, Gogol was still rationalising his intention some ten years later, when he even proposed an allegorical interpretation. In an essay written in 1846, Gogol claimed that his provincial town in fact symbolised the human spirit, and its various characters represented our ungoverned passions. Khlestakov acted as its conscience, but one itself corrupted by society, while the real inspector stood for the true conscience of man, awakened only at the point of death. This is at some remove from the 'authentic Russian anecdote' he begged from Pushkin in 1835, and arguably even further removed from an audience's actual experience of the play.

However, while we may believe that Gogol's astonishment at how its first audience interpreted the work was a little naive, he was also angered, with more justice perhaps, by the manner of its performance. Gogol's characters are embroiled in a farcical siuation, but they are not mere caricatures; they are recognizable human types, their vices exaggerated as dominant character traits, overlaid with a rich patina of detail. Coarse acting, playing to the gallery, can dehumanize them, and that appears to have been the case at its première in 1836, when the key role of Khlestakov, taken by an actor called Dür, was self-consciously played for laughs.

At any rate, Gogol was eventually compelled to write a set of instructions, which are still relevant today. The actor, he says, must first find the 'common humanity' of his role, and identify what drives the character. At all costs he must avoid overstatement, and should instead appear almost oblivious of the audience, entirely wrapped up in his own concerns. Essentially, *The Government Inspector* will take its tone in performance from

Khlestakov and the Mayor, and Gogol is at pains to stress that Khlestakov is not a simple impostor, but a virtuoso fantasist, who deludes himself as enthusiastically as he does his provincial hosts. Nor is the Mayor, venal and self-seeking as he may be, a mere scoundrel. Rather, he regards the use of power for personal gain as entirely natural, blind to everything but the main chance.

Gogol accordingly argues for a three-dimensional reading, and this is also clear in his detailed notes on the characters and their costumes:

> The Mayor: a man grown old in the service, and in his own way extremely shrewd. Despite his bribe-taking, he conducts himself with dignity; grave in demeanour, even rather sententious; speaks neither loudly or softly, neither too much nor too little. His every word is significant. His features are coarse and hard, someone who has worked his way up from the ranks. Rapid transitions from fear to joy, from servility to arrogance, reveal a man of crudely developed instincts. Routinely dressed in official uniform, with braided facings, top-boots and spurs. Short grizzled hair.

> Anna Andreevna: his wife, a provincial coquette of a certain age, educated partly out of romantic novels and album verse, and partly from bustling around, overseeing the pantry and the maids' room. She is extremely inquisitive, and displays her vanity at every turn. Occasionally has the upper hand over her husband, but only when he is stuck for a reply, and her dominance extends no further than trivial matters, expressed in nagging and mockery. She has four complete changes of costume in the course of the play.

> Khlestakov: a young man of about twenty-three, slim-built, almost skinny; a little scatterbrained, with, as they say, not a great deal upstairs; one of those people in government service referred to as 'nitwits'. Speaks and acts without a thought. Quite incapable of concentrating on any particular idea. His delivery is rather staccato, and he says the first thing that comes into his head. The more naivety and simplicity the

actor brings to this role, the more successful he will be. Dressed in the height of fashion.

Osip: his manservant, like the generality of servants who are getting on in years: sober-sided, eyes downcast most of the time; something of a moraliser, fond of repeating little maxims to himself, but for the benefit of his master. His voice is almost always level, but in conversation with Khlestakov occasionally takes on a harsh, abrupt tone, to the point of rudeness. He is more intelligent than his master, and thus quicker on the uptake, but doesn't say much, and craftily keeps his own counsel. Wears a shabby grey or dark blue coat.

Bobchinsky and Dobchinsky: both men are short and squat and intensely inquisitive; their resemblance to one another is quite extraordinary; both have little pot-bellies, both gabble at high speed, helped along by gestures and hand-waving. Dobchinsky is slightly taller and more sedate than Bobchinsky, but the latter is jollier and more animated.

Lyapkin-Tyapkin: the Judge, a man who has read five or six books and fancies himself a freethinker. Much given to conjecture, he weighs carefully his every word. The actor playing him must maintain a portentous expression at all times. Speaks in a deep bass voice, with a drawling delivery, and a throaty wheeze, like one of those antique clocks that hiss before they strike.

Zemlyanika: the Charities Warden, a rather fat, sluggish and cumbersome person, but a sly rogue nonetheless. Extremely servile and officious.

Postmaster: simpleminded to the point of naivety.

The other roles need no explanation. Their originals can be seen almost everywhere.

The actors should pay close attention to the concluding tableau. The final lines should produce an immediate electrifying effect on all present, and the entire cast must adopt its new position instantly. A cry of astonishment must erupt from all the women simultaneously, as if from a single pair of lungs. Failure to observe these notes may ruin the whole effect.

One can imagine Gogol's chagrin at seeing the Khlestakov described above travestied by Dür as a professional confidence trickster, and even though the play was staged the following month in Moscow, with a new cast which included the great Mikhail Shchepkin as the Mayor, the Maly Theatre actors, soon to become skilled interpreters of Ostrovsky, were still too broad for Gogol's taste. Nonetheless, *The Government Inspector* speedily entered the permanent repertoire, where it has remained ever since. In 1921, for example, in a key production by the Moscow Art Theatre, directed by Stanislavsky, Mikhail Chekhov (the nephew of Anton) is said to have played Khlestakov as a pathological liar, perhaps closer to Gogol's ideal.

Other notable Khlestakovs include the American comedian Danny Kaye, in a Hollywood musical adaptation of 1949, and Paul Scofield in a 1966 RSC production, directed by Peter Hall. Ian Richardson recreated the role at the Old Vic in 1979, and more recently, the television comic Rik Mayall played Khlestakov in a National Theatre production, directed by Richard Eyre in 1985.

Since its first staging, however, arguably the most striking production was that of Vsevolod Meyerhold in 1926, using a text enlarged by extracts from Gogol's prose works, and which lasted four hours. Against a semi-circular array of imposing double doors, Meyerhold divided *The Government Inspector* up into fifteen episodes, with specially commissioned music, and not only reinforced the play's pantomime elements, but also its darker satire. For Meyerhold, Gogol's real target was not an isolated abuse of power in some remote outpost of Nicholas I's empire, but the entire régime. Controversial as the production was, not least because of the liberties taken with Gogol's text, it remained a fixture in the repertoire until 1938, when Stalin ordered the liquidation first of Meyerhold's theatre, then of the director himself.

In his own lifetime, Gogol was never reconciled to his creation, and the allegorical *dénouement*, which he proposed staging as a sort of epilogue in 1846, was quite properly dismissed by his friends as an aberration. Like all great fiction, Gogol's master-piece exhausts interpretation, even that of its creator. Near the end of his life, the author morosely offered his own assessment of what he had achieved:

> In *The Government Inspector* I resolved to gather into one heap everything that was bad in Russia, which I was aware of at that time, all the injustices being perpetrated in those places, and in those circumstances that especially cried out for justice, and tried to hold them all up to ridicule, at one fell swoop. However, as is well known, that produced a tremendous effect. Through the laughter, which I had never before vented with such force, the reader could feel my deep sorrow...

Gogol's sombre reflections, however, tell us little about the workings of this superbly crafted comedy, which continues to delight audiences everywhere, transcending the limitations of its own period and culture. Nabokov describes it as the greatest play ever written in Russian, and the key to its success perhaps lies in the 'common humanity' Gogol attempted to urge on its first clumsy interpreters. In the words of the Mayor, traditionally spoken facing the audience:

> 'So what are you laughing at, eh? You're laughing at yourselves, that's what!'

The Translation

The American poet William Carlos Williams once observed that: 'the only true universal resides in the local and particular', and Gogol's great universal comedy is intensely specific to its own culture. This is nowhere more obvious than in the complex administrative arrangements of his provincial town, and the translator is thus faced with the problem of finding English equivalents for uniquely Russian institutions.

Among the most important of these is the so-called Table of Ranks. This was a system introduced by Peter the Great in 1722, which classified civil servants into fourteen grades, on a par with commissioned ranks in the military, and virtually everyone, save petty traders and serfs, was positioned on this social ladder. Much of the piquancy of relationships in 19th-century Russian fiction derives from it, and it is interesting to note that Gogol himself, on his arrival in St Petersburg, held the rank of 'collegiate registrar', i.e., the 14th grade, equivalent to a cornet or ensign. In *The Government Inspector*, this is Khlestakov's rank.

Furthermore, while all ranks were regarded as belonging to the nobility, only the first eight were hereditary, and superiors were addressed in accordance with the precise position they occupied in the hierarchy. In Act III of *The Government Inspector*, the characters formally introduce themselves by name, post and rank: thus, the Judge is a collegiate assessor, 8th grade, equivalent to a major; the Postmaster is a court councillor, 7th grade, equivalent to a lieutenant-colonel; the Mayor himself, the town's leading citizen, holds the rank of collegiate councillor, 6th grade, equivalent to a colonel.

In translation, I have generally left these intact, with the occasional exception, and one such occurs in Osip's Act II soliloquy, when, scornful of his master's pretensions, he dismisses him as a 'jumped-up clerk'. The Russian here is *elistratishka prostoi*, literally, a 'simple collegiate registrar', but the uneducated Osip manages only a garbled version of Khlestakov's title in any case. Elsewhere, forms of address are not always translated in strict accordance with the Table of Ranks, and the use of first name and patronymic, and also diminutives, so common in Russian still, has been much reduced, for ease of speaking in English. Gogol gets some comic mileage out of the fact that Bobchinsky and Dobchinsky are both 'Pyotr Ivanovich', for example, but I have used their surnames for the most part.

Russian names, with their unfamiliar consonant clusters, are problematic at the best of times, and notes on pronunciation are here given in an Appendix, on page 101. *The Government Inspector* is made even more difficult in this respect, however, by Gogol's taste for loading his characters' names with comic significance. Thus, the Mayor rejoices in the absurd family name of 'Skvoznik-Dmukhanovsky', which suggests a draught of air, literally, but has figurative overtones of sharp practice and social climbing; Judge Lyapkin-Tyapkin is fittingly labelled 'slapdash'; Postmaster Shpyokin, it is suggested, is a 'snooper'; Khlopov, the Schools Superintendent, derives his name from the verb 'to make a dull thud'; Zemlyanika, the Charities Warden, is literally 'a strawberry'; and Constables Svistunov, Derzhimorda, Pugovitsyn, and Police Chief Ukhovyortov are related to words meaning respectively: 'to whistle', 'to shut one's trap', 'to frighten' (also 'a button'), and 'to twist an ear'. Gogol maintains this device through the entire cast, seen and unseen, and Khlestakov's journalist crony, e.g., Tryapichkin, takes his name from *tryapki*, 'rags'. Khlestakov himself, despatched from the capital, it is believed, to whip these corrupt and indolent provincials into line, is named from a verb whose primary meaning is 'to lash', but as Nabokov observes, a Russian ear also picks up a wide range of echoes, from the swish of a cane to the slap of playing cards. Regrettably, short of giving the characters fantastical English names, such nuances are impossible to convey, though they are useful as background, and I have again opted for ease of playing.

There is a further problem concerning the various posts Gogol's provincials occupy. The Mayor, for example, translates here the Russian *gorodnichy*, appointed by the government chiefly to maintain public order, but also responsible for the upkeep of roads, bridges, etc. 'Prefect' might thus be more accurate, but 'mayor' is hallowed by tradition. The duties of the Postmaster include overseeing the hire of horses, etc., as well as the transmission of letters, but while those of the Judge and Schools Superintendent are broadly self-explanatory, the Charities Warden's remit is more complex. Zemlyanika's full title is 'Guardian of Charitable Insitutions', and he is answerable to a government body such as the Board of Public Charity, set up in the reign of Catherine the Great, to administer orphanages, hospitals, workhouses, etc., and authorised to act as a form of trustee savings bank, for fundraising purposes. There is a markedly Dickensian note about the institution, but no exact English equivalent, at least not which can be succinctly expressed.

Finally, Gogol takes pains to differentiate the speech of his characters, ranging from the Mayor's curious mixture of pomposity and vulgarity, the mark of the self-made man, to the novelettish vapourings of his wife and daughter; from Osip's earthy downrightness, to Khlestakov's city slicker patter, and the freakish circumlocutions of the two Pyotr Ivanoviches. *The Government Inspector* is a rare achievement of language and comic invention, and no translator can do more than attempt yet another faint echo of Gogol's masterpiece.

Stephen Mulrine,
Glasgow 1996

For Further Reading

Among the more general works, Henri Troyat's *Gogol: the Biography of a Divided Soul*, translated by Nancy Amphoux (George Allen & Unwin, 1974), is both informative and absorbing, and Vladimir Nabokov's 1944 study, *Nikolay Gogol* (re-issued, Weidenfeld & Nicolson 1974), offers an individual perspective which has lost none of its vigour.

For contextual purposes, *Russian Theatre: from Empire to Soviets*, by Marc Slonim (Methuen, 1961) is useful, and the influential Meyerhold production is analysed at length in *The Theatre of Meyerhold: Revolution on the Modern Stage*, by Edward Braun (Eyre Methuen, 1979). It is also the subject of a fascinating reconstruction by Nick Worrell in *Theatre Quarterly*, Vol. II, No. 7, 1972.

Gogol From the Twentieth Century (Princeton University Press, 1974), is a collection of key Russian and Soviet essays on Gogol, edited and translated by Robert A Maguire, while the same author's *Exploring Gogol* (Stanford University Press, 1994), and Simon Karlinsky's *The Sexual Labyrinth of Nikolai Gogol* (Cambridge, Mass., 1976) make an interesting contribution to the debate surrounding the writer's state of mind.

Gogol: Key Dates

1809   Born March 20th, in the market town of Sorochintsy, in Mirgorod province.

1828   Graduates from high school at Nezhin, moves to St Petersburg.

1829   June: publishes *Hans Küchelgarten*. Following hostile reviews, leaves for Germany. Returns to St Petersburg in September, obtains civil service post.

1831   January: appointed to teach history at the Patriotic Institute, a young ladies' college. September: publishes first volume of *Evenings on a Farm near Dikanka*.

1832   March: publishes second volume.

1834   July: appointed assistant professor of history at St Petersburg University.

1835   January: publishes *Arabesques*, including *The Portrait, Nevsky Prospect*, and *Diary of a Madman*. March: publishes *Mirgorod*, two volumes, including *Taras Bulba*, and *The Quarrel of the Two Ivans*. December: quits teaching, begins work on *Dead Souls*, completes *The Government Inspector*.

1836   April 19th: first performance of *The Government Inspector*, at Alexandrinsky Theatre, St Petersburg. May 25th: first performance at Maly Theatre, Moscow. June: leaves Russia, to tour Europe. October: *The Nose* published in Pushkin's journal 'The Contemporary'.

1837   March: settles in Rome.

1842   April: publishes first volume of *Dead Souls*.

1843   Publication of *Collected Works*, in four volumes, including *The Overcoat*, hitherto unpublished. February: *Marriage* and *The Gamblers* performed in Moscow.

1845   July: destroys manuscript of *Dead Souls, Part II*.

1847   Publication of *Selected Passages from Correspondence with Friends*. Comes under influence of archpriest Father Matvei, spiritual adviser.

1848   January: Gogol sets out on pilgrimage to Jerusalem. May: returns to Russia.

1852   February 11th: destroys revised version of *Dead Souls, Part II*. February 21st: dies in Moscow.

Dates are given 'Old Style', i.e., according to the Julian calendar, used in Russia until 1918, roughly eleven days behind the modern Gregorian calendar.

THE GOVERNMENT INSPECTOR

If your face is twisted, it's no use blaming the mirror.

Popular saying

Dramatis Personae

SKVOZNIK-DMUKHANOVSKY, *a provincial Mayor*
ANNA, *his wife*
MARYA, *his daughter*
KHLOPOV, *a Superintendent of Schools*
His wife
LYAPKIN-TYAPKIN, *a Judge*
ZEMLYANIKA, *a Charities Warden*
SHPYOKIN, *a Postmaster*
DOBCHINSKY, *a local landowner*
BOBCHINSKY, *a local landowner*
KHLESTAKOV, *a St. Petersburg clerk*
OSIP, *his manservant*
GIBNER, *a local landowner*
LYULYUKOV, *a retired civil servant, and local dignitary*
RASTAKOVSKY, *a retired civil servant, and local dignitary*
KOROBKIN, *a retired civil servant, and local dignitary*
UKHOVYORTOV, *Chief of Police*
SVISTUNOV, *a police constable*
PUGOVITSYN, *a police constable*
DERZHIMORDA, *a police constable*
ABDULIN, *a merchant*
POSHLYOPKINA, *Fevronya, a locksmith's wife*
A Sergeant's wife
MISHKA, *the Mayor's manservant*
A waiter at the inn
Guests, merchants, townsfolk, petitioners

Pronunciation: see Appendix, page 101

Act One

A room in the MAYOR's *house. The* MAYOR, CHARITIES
WARDEN, SCHOOLS SUPERINTENDENT, JUDGE,
PHYSICIAN, *and two* CONSTABLES.

MAYOR. Gentlemen, I have invited you here to inform you of
some extremely unpleasant news: we are about to receive an
Inspector.

JUDGE. An inspector?

WARDEN. What sort of inspector?

MAYOR. A Government Inspector from St. Petersburg,
travelling incognito. With secret instructions, no less.

JUDGE. Oh dear!

WARDEN. That's the last thing we need!

SUPERINTENDENT. Good Lord! Secret instructions!

MAYOR. You know, I had a premonition: the whole of last
night I kept dreaming about two extraordinary rats. I tell
you, I've never seen anything like it: huge, black things,
monsters. They came up and started sniffing around, then
cleared off. I'll read you this letter, which I've just received
from Andrei Ivanovich – I think you know him, Warden.
Anyway, this is what he says: 'My dear friend, godfather,
and benefactor . . . ' (*Muttering under his breath as he scans the
paper.*) ' . . . to inform you that . . . ' Ah, here it is: 'Meanwhile, I hasten to inform you that an official has just arrived
with orders to inspect the whole province, and in particular,
our district . . . (*Holds up a finger, meaningfully.*) . . . I have this
on the most reliable authority, although he is passing himself
off as a private citizen. So, as I know you have your little

vices like the rest of us, being a sensible chap, who never lets anything slip through his fingers . . . ' (*Stops.*) Well, we're among friends here . . . ' . . . I advise you to take precautions. He may arrive at any time, if indeed he hasn't arrived already and is staying incognito somewhere . . . Yesterday afternoon I . . . ' Ah, now he goes on to family business: 'Cousin Anna paid us a visit with her husband; Cousin Ivan has got very stout, but can still play the fiddle . . . ' et cetera, et cetera. So there we are, gentlemen, that's the situation.

JUDGE. Yes, it's a most unusual situation – most unusual. There's something behind it.

SUPERINTENDENT. But why, Mister Mayor? What on earth for? And why us?

MAYOR. Why? It's fate, obviously! (*Sighs.*) Until now, thanks be to God, they've poked around in other towns. Now it's our turn.

JUDGE. Well, I fancy we're seeing some quite subtle *realpolitik* here, Mister Mayor. I think it means that Russia . . . Yes, that's it, we're going to declare war, and the Government, you see, have sent out this official, to check for treason.

MAYOR. Oh, don't be ridiculous! And you're supposed to be clever? Treason, in this neck of the woods, really! It's not as if we're on the frontier, are we? Good God, you could gallop out of here for three years, and still not reach a foreign country!

JUDGE. No, seriously . . . You don't know . . . I mean . . . They have some extremely shrewd ideas, the Government. Distance doesn't come into it, they keep their eyes peeled just the same.

MAYOR. Well, eyes peeled or unpeeled, don't say I haven't warned you, gentlemen. As you'll see, I've made certain arrangements in my own department, and I advise you to do likewise. Especially you, Warden! Beyond a shadow of a doubt, the first thing any visiting official will want to inspect is your charity institutions, so you'd better get them into decent order: clean night-caps, for a start. We don't want the patients looking like coal-miners, the way they usually go about.

WARDEN. That's all right. I dare say we can stick clean night-caps on them.

MAYOR. Good. Oh, and hang a notice in Latin or something above each bed – this is your department now, Doctor – the name of the illness, when they took sick, the day of the week and month . . . And it's not a good idea letting patients smoke that foul tobacco, so you start coughing and spluttering the minute you go in there. Yes, and you'd better discharge a few: otherwise they'll put it down to bad management or the Doctor's incompetence.

WARDEN. Well, really! Dr Gibner and I have our own system, that's all. As far as treatment's concerned, the closer to Nature the better. That's why we don't bother with expensive medicines. Man is a simple creature: if he's going to die, he'll die; if he's going to recover, he'll recover. Actually, the Doctor would have trouble communicating with them anyway – he doesn't speak a word of Russian.

The PHYSICIAN utters a sound, mid-way between 'ee' and 'eh'.

MAYOR. And I'd advise you, Judge, to do something about that court-house of yours. The watchmen keep geese in the hall, where the clients are supposed to go, and the goslings are getting under people's feet. All right, poultry-farming's a thoroughly respectable business – why shouldn't the watch-men engage in it? But it's not decent, in a court-house. I ought to have mentioned that before, only it slipped my mind.

JUDGE. Fine, I'll have the lot whipped off into the kitchen today. You can come to dinner, if you like.

MAYOR. What's more, it isn't very nice hanging all sorts of rubbish up to dry in the courtroom, and dumping your riding tackle on top of the document chest. I know you're keen on hunting and all that, but you'd better keep it out of sight for a while. You can hang it back up again, once the Inspector's moved on. And that clerk of yours . . . well, I dare say he knows his job, but he smells as if he'd emerged straight from a distillery – that's not very nice, either. I've been meaning to have a word with you about that too, but I got sidetracked somehow, I don't remember. Anyway, there's surely something he can take for that, if, as he says, it's just his natural odour. You should tell him to eat onions, or garlic, or something. In fact, the Doctor might be of use here, with those medicines of his.

The PHYSICIAN *utters the same curious sound.*

JUDGE. No, he can't get rid of it. He says his nurse dropped him when he was a baby and he's given off a slight whiff of vodka ever since.

MAYOR. Well, it was just a thought. As far as your internal arrangements go, and what Andrei Ivanovich calls our little vices, what can I say? You know, it's a strange thing, but there's nobody who hasn't got some kind of sin to answer. After all, that's how the good Lord made us, no matter what these freethinkers say.

JUDGE. And just exactly what do you mean by little vices, Mister Mayor? Surely there are vices and vices? I tell people quite openly that I accept bribes, but what sort of bribes, eh? Greyhound pups, that's all.

MAYOR. It doesn't matter if it's pups or whatever, it's still bribery.

JUDGE. No, not at all, Mister Mayor. For instance, if a certain person accepts a fur coat worth five hundred roubles, and his wife gets a shawl . . .

MAYOR. Yes, well, you needn't think your greyhound pups'll save you! You don't believe in God, for a start. And you never go to church. At least I've still got my faith, and go to church every Sunday. Whereas you – you've only got to start talking about the Creation, and it's enough to make a person's hair stand on end.

JUDGE. Well, that's the conclusion I've come to, thinking it out for myself.

MAYOR. You know, in some cases, too many brains can be worse than none. Anyway, I only mentioned the court-house in passing; I shouldn't think anybody'll want to look in there, frankly. You're lucky with that place, it must be under the Lord's special protection. Now, Superintendent, as overseer of our educational establishments, you'll need to take particular care with the schoolteachers. Of course, they're educated people, they've been trained at all sorts of colleges, but they've got some very strange ways – I suppose they acquire them along with their scholarly vocation. One of them, for instance, that one with the fat chops, I can't remember his name – every time he's up on the platform he pulls the most awful face, like this, (*Grimaces.*) and then starts smoothing out his beard, with his hand under his cravat. All right, let him make faces like that at the pupils, that's neither here nor there. Maybe he can't help it, I'm not in a position to say. But you just imagine, if he does that to a visitor, it could be disastrous. This Inspector or whoever might take it personally. And God only knows what might come of that.

SUPERINTENDENT. Yes, but what am I supposed to do with him? I've told him about it often enough. Just the other day, our Marshal happened to drop into his classroom, and he screwed up his face into the most terrifying grimace, like nothing I've ever seen in my life. He didn't mean any harm, I daresay, but I got a dressing-down for allowing our young people to be infected with subversive ideas.

MAYOR. There's that history teacher of yours, too. He has a good head on him, that's obvious, a positive mine of information, but when he's explaining something he gets completely carried away. I listened to him once – he was fine on the Assyrians and Babylonians, but the minute he reached

Alexander the Great, I tell you, it was indescribable. Ye gods, I thought the place was on fire! He ran down off the platform and banged his chair on the floor, full force! All right, Alexander the Great is a hero, but why smash up the furniture? It all comes out of the public purse, you know.

SUPERINTENDENT. Well, he *is* an enthusiast. I've mentioned it on several occasions, but all he says is, 'Do what you like, I won't spare myself in the cause of learning.'

MAYOR. It's like some mysterious natural law: these scholarly types either drink like fish, or else they pull such awful faces you've got to take the holy icons out of the room!

SUPERINTENDENT. Well, God help anybody in the education business! You're frightened the whole time, people all have to poke their noses in, everybody wants to show they're as clever as you.

MAYOR. I wouldn't care if it weren't for that damned incognito! But he'll suddenly pop up: 'Ah, there you are, my dear chaps!' he'll say, 'And who's the District Judge hereabouts?' 'Lyapkin-Tyapkin.' 'Right then, bring me Lyapkin-Tyapkin! And who's the Charities Warden?' 'Zemlyanika.' 'Right, bring me Zemlyanika!' That's the worst part!

The POSTMASTER *enters.*

POSTMASTER. Gentlemen, gentlemen, tell me, please – what's going on, what's all this about an Inspector?

MAYOR. You haven't heard?

POSTMASTER. Only just now from Bobchinsky. He was in my post office a minute ago.

MAYOR. Well then, what do you think?

POSTMASTER. What do I think? It's war with the Turks, it must be.

JUDGE. Exactly what I said. Great minds think alike.

MAYOR. Yes, and fools seldom differ.

POSTMASTER. War with the Turks, definitely. It's the French stirring things up again.

MAYOR. What are you talking about, war with the Turks? It's us that are going to cop it, not the Turks. We know what it's about – I've got a letter here.

POSTMASTER. Oh well, in that case, it can't be war with the Turks.

MAYOR. So tell us, Postmaster, what do you make of it?

POSTMASTER. Me? Why me? What about you, Mister Mayor?

MAYOR. What do you mean me? I've nothing to fear – not much, anyway. Though I'm a bit worried about the business people and townsfolk, of course. They'll say I've been hard on them, but I swear to God if I've taken anything from anybody, there was no malice in it. Actually, I'm beginning to wonder . . . (*Takes the* POSTMASTER *by the arm and draws him aside.*) I'm beginning to wonder if somebody might not have reported me. I mean, why on earth should we get an Inspector? Listen, Postmaster, couldn't you just . . . for the common good, obviously . . . couldn't you just stop every letter that passes through your post office, incoming or outgoing, and well . . . melt the seal a tiny bit? You know, to see if it contains anything like a report, or if it's just routine correspondence? Obviously, if there's nothing in it, you can seal it up again, or deliver it unsealed, for that matter.

POSTMASTER. Yes, I know, I know. There's nothing you can teach me on that score. I do it all the time, not so much as a precaution, as out of curiosity. I like to know what's going on in the world. It makes fascinating reading, I can tell you. Some of these letters are a joy to read, the way they describe events – a real education, better than the 'Moscow Gazette'!

MAYOR. So, you haven't picked up anything about some official from St. Petersburg?

POSTMASTER. No, nothing about St. Petersburg, though there's a lot of talk about officials in Kostroma and Saratov.

It's a pity you can't read those letters, though – there are some lovely passages in them. There was a lieutenant the other day writing to a friend, describing some ball he'd been at, in the most lively manner . . . it was extremely well done: 'My dear friend,' he says, 'I pass my life here in transports of delight, young ladies galore, the band playing, the colours flying . . . ' Really, he described it all with such feeling. I've hung onto that one deliberately. Would you like to read it?

MAYOR. No, there's no time for that. Anyway, if you'd do me the kindness, Postmaster – anything that turns up, by way of a complaint or report, don't hesitate to hold it back.

POSTMASTER. My pleasure.

JUDGE. You'd better watch out – one of these days you'll cop it for this.

POSTMASTER. Heaven forfend!

MAYOR. It's all right, don't worry. It'd be a different case if you were making any of it public, but this is a family matter.

JUDGE. Even so, that's a nasty business you're involved in. Incidentally, Mister Mayor, I was just coming over to make you a present of a bitch pup. She's the blood sister to that dog I've told you about. You'll have heard, of course, that Cheptovich and Varkhovinsky are suing each other now, so I'm in clover: I can chase after the hares on both their lands.

MAYOR. Ye gods, what do I want with your hares? I've got that damned incognito preying on my mind. I'm expecting a door to open any second, and wham!

Enter BOBCHINSKY *and* DOBCHINSKY, *out of breath.*

BOBCHINSKY. Extraordinary occurrence!

DOBCHINSKY. Unexpected news!

ALL. What is it? What is it?

DOBCHINSKY. Unforeseen development. We go into the tavern . . .

BOBCHINSKY (*interrupting*). Yes, Dobchinsky and I go into the tavern . . .

DOBCHINSKY (*interrupting*). Excuse me, Bobchinsky – I'm telling the story . . .

BOBCHINSKY. No, no, let me tell it . . . Allow me . . . You haven't got the knack for it . . .

DOBCHINSKY. You'll get all mixed up, and you'll miss something out.

BOBCHINSKY. I won't, I won't, honestly! Now, don't interfere, let me get on with it. Gentlemen, please, kindly tell Dobchinsky not to interfere.

MAYOR. Look, for God's sake, tell us what's going on! I'm having palpitations here. Sit down, gentlemen! Bring some chairs! Here, Bobchinsky, take a seat. (*They all sit down, grouped round* BOBCHINSKY *and* DOBCHINSKY.) Well, come on, tell us.

BOBCHINSKY. Please, allow me . . . I'll tell it all in order. Right then . . . just after I'd had the pleasure of leaving your house, sir, when you had been somewhat troubled, indeed, sir, by the receipt of a certain letter . . . well, at that point I dashed off to . . . no, don't interrupt, Dobchinsky! I've got the whole story, sirs, absolutely all of it. Anyway, as it happens, sir, I hurried round to Korobkin's place. And not finding Korobkin at home, I looked in on Rastakovsky, and when I couldn't find Rastakovsky, why then, I went round to the Postmaster's, to inform him of the news you'd just received, sir, and on my way back, I bumped into Dobchinsky here . . .

DOBCHINSKY (*interrupting*). Yes, near that stall where they sell the pies.

BOBCHINSKY. Where they sell the pies. Anyway, I bumped into Dobchinsky and I said to him, 'Well, have you heard the news our good Mayor has just received in a letter from a reliable source?' And Dobchinsky had already heard about it from your housekeeper Avdotya, sir, who had been sent round to Filipp Antonovich, I've no idea what for.

DOBCHINSKY (*interrupting*). A keg of French brandy.

BOBCHINSKY (*waving him aside*). A keg of French brandy. So, off Dobchinsky and I go to see Filipp Antonovich . . . Look here, Dobchinsky – don't interrupt, please don't do that! . . . We set off for Filipp Antonovich's, and on the way Dobchinsky says, 'Let's drop into the tavern,' he says, 'It's my stomach, I haven't had a thing since breakfast, my stomach's rumbling . . . ' Yes, it was Dobchinsky's stomach at the root of it. 'They've just had a delivery of fresh salmon,' he says, 'We can have a bite to eat.' So, we've no sooner sat down, when this young man . . .

DOBCHINSKY (*interrupting*). Not at all bad-looking, and wearing an ordinary suit . . .

BOBCHINSKY. Not at all bad-looking, and wearing an ordinary suit, walks into the room, like so, with a sort of thoughtful, discerning expression on his face – and obviously a lot going on up here . . . (*Taps his forehead.*) Anyway, I have a kind of presentiment, and I say to Dobchinsky, 'Well, sir, there's more here than meets the eye.' Yes, indeed. But Dobchinsky's already signalled to the innkeeper – Vlas, his name is, actually. His wife gave birth three weeks ago, a lively little chap. He'll be an innkeeper just like his father. Anyway, we call Vlas over and Dobchinsky asks him very quietly, 'Who's that young man?' he says. 'Well,' says Vlas, 'That's . . . ' Dobchinsky, please don't interrupt. It's not you that's telling the story, so don't keep butting in. You've got a lisp, as I happen to know, and you whistle through your teeth. Anyway, Vlas says he's a civil servant, he says, on his way from St. Petersburg, he says, and his name's Khlestakov, he says, headed for Saratov province, he says, and his behaviour's most peculiar: he's been there two weeks already, he says, never leaves the inn, gets everything on tick and won't pay a penny. And while he's telling me all this, it suddenly dawned on me. 'Aha!' I says to Dobchinsky . . .

DOBCHINSKY. No, Bobchinsky, it was me that said, 'Aha!'

BOBCHINSKY. All right then, you said it first, but I said it afterwards. 'Aha!' we both said, Dobchinsky and I, 'Why's he hanging about here, when he's supposed to be on his way to Saratov?' Yes, indeed, sirs. So, there you have it – he's the one!

MAYOR. Who is? What one?

BOBCHINSKY. He's the civil servant you got the letter about – the Inspector.

MAYOR (*in terror*). God almighty, it can't be!

DOBCHINSKY. It's him! He doesn't pay any money, he doesn't go anywhere. Who else could it be? And he's got an official order for post-horses to Saratov.

BOBCHINSKY. It's him, it must be. I mean, he was looking at everything, he misses nothing. He spotted Dobchinsky and me eating salmon – mainly because Dobchinsky's stomach had been . . . well, anyway, he came up and gave our plates the once-over. Put the fear of God into me, I can tell you.

MAYOR. Lord have mercy on us sinners! What room is he staying in?

DOBCHINSKY. Number Five, under the stairs.

BOBCHINSKY. That's the room those officers had the fight in last year.

MAYOR. Has he been here long?

DOBCHINSKY. Two weeks. He arrived here on St. Basil the Egyptian's Day.

MAYOR. Two whole weeks! Good God Almighty! Take the holy icons out before I start swearing! These two weeks the Sergeant's wife's been flogged! The convicts haven't had their rations! The streets are filthy, the whole town's like a dungheap! It's a disgrace! (*Clutches his head.*)

WARDEN. What'll we do, Mister Mayor? March over to the tavern in a body?

JUDGE. No, no! We should send the Mayor in first, then the clergy, then the business community – you know, same as in that book, 'The Acts of John the Freemason' . . .

MAYOR. No no, leave it to me. I've got out of some tricky situations before this, yes, and been thanked for my pains. Maybe the good Lord'll get me out of this one too. (*Turns to* BOBCHINSKY.) You say he's a young chap?

BOBCHINSKY. Yes, twenty-three or twenty-four at most.

MAYOR. So much the better. Young people are easier to size up. It'd be a disaster if it was some old devil – young people you can read like a book. Right then, gentlemen, make everything ready in your own departments, and I'll go for a little stroll on my own, or possibly with Dobchinsky here – unofficially, of course – to make sure we're not mistreating our guests. Hey, Svistunov!

SVISTUNOV. Yes, sir!

MAYOR. Get me the Chief of Police, right away – no, on second thoughts, I need you here. Tell somebody outside to fetch him, and then come back. (*The* CONSTABLE *dashes off.*)

WARDEN. Come on, Judge, let's go! We could be in serious trouble here.

JUDGE. I don't know what you're worried about. Dish out some clean night-caps and that's the end of it.

WARDEN. What do you mean, night-caps? I was told to give the patients oatmeal gruel, and the stink of cabbage in the corridors is so bad you have to hold your nose.

JUDGE. Well, that doesn't bother me. Who's going to come into a District Court? But if he looks at any of the paperwork, my life won't be worth living. Fifteen years I've been on the Bench now, and when I have to consult the

Court records, well, I throw up my hands in despair.
Solomon himself couldn't sort out truth from fiction in those.

The JUDGE, *the* CHARITIES WARDEN, *the* SCHOOLS
SUPERINTENDENT, *and the* POSTMASTER *all exit,
colliding with the returning* CONSTABLE *in the doorway.*

MAYOR. Well, is my droshky ready?

CONSTABLE. Yes, sir.

MAYOR. Right, go outside and . . . no, wait! Run and fetch
my . . . Where all the others? Are you on your own? I
distinctly told Prokhorov to be here. Where's Prokhorov?

CONSTABLE. Prokhorov's at the station-house, sir, but he
won't be much use for this business.

MAYOR. What do you mean?

CONSTABLE. Well, sir, he was dead to the world when they
carried him in this morning. They've poured two tubs of cold
water over him already, and he still hasn't sobered up.

MAYOR (*clutching his head*). Oh, my God! Look, run outside . . .
no, don't, go to my room first, d'you hear? Fetch me my
sword and my new hat! Let's go, Dobchinsky!

BOBCHINSKY. And me too, Mister Mayor, me too!

MAYOR. No, no, Bobchinsky, you can't! It's too awkward, we
won't all fit in the droshky.

BOBCHINSKY. Right then, I don't care – I'll run along
behind it, I'll just tag along. I only want to peep through a
tiny chink in the door, just to see what he's like . . .

MAYOR (*to the* CONSTABLE, *taking his sword*). Now, hurry and
round up all the other constables, and tell them to get hold
of a . . . Oh Lord, this sword's scratched! That damned
Abdulin – he can see the Mayor's sword's worn out but he
can't send me a new one! Honestly, a pack of rogues! Yes,
and I bet those swindlers are busy honing up their complaints
right now. Anyway, tell the constables to go outside and pick

up a . . . dammit, go out on the street, with a brush, right?
Sweep the whole street, all the way up to the inn, and make
sure it's clean, d'you hear? And you watch out – yes, you!
I know you too well – you're as thick as thieves with that
lot, you'll be in there, slipping the silver teaspoons down
your boot-tops. Just watch your step, I've got sharp ears,
you know! What did you do to Chernyaev, the draper, eh?
He was giving you two yards of cloth for a tunic, and you
whipped the whole roll. So watch it – don't overstep the
mark. Right, clear off!

The CHIEF OF POLICE *enters.*

MAYOR. Stepan! For heaven's sake, where've you disappeared
to? How d'you think that looks, eh?

POLICE CHIEF. I've been right here, at the gates.

MAYOR. Stepan, listen – there's an official arrived from St.
Petersburg. What arrangements have you made?

POLICE CHIEF. I've done as you ordered. I've sent Constable
Pugovitsyn with a squad to clean up the pavements.

MAYOR. What about Derzhimorda? Where's he?

POLICE CHIEF. He's gone out with the fire-pump.

MAYOR. And Prokhorov's drunk.

POLICE CHIEF. That's right.

MAYOR. How could you let that happen?

POLICE CHIEF. God knows. There was a fight outside the
town yesterday afternoon – he went to sort it out, and came
back drunk.

MAYOR. Anyway, listen, this is what you've got to do:
Pugovitsyn's a tall chap, you can stand him on the bridge,
he'll show to advantage there. And you can pull down that
old fence, the one beside the cobbler's shop, and put out
some straw markers, so it'll look like a building-site. The
more things we pull down the better, it shows the adminis-

tration's active. Oh, my God, I nearly forgot! There's a mountain of rubbish at the back of that fence, must be about forty cart-loads of it. What a disgusting dump this town is! The minute you put up any kind of monument, or even a plain fence, they pile all sorts of rubbish against it, heaven knows where it comes from! (*Sighs.*) Yes, and if this Inspector asks your police if they're happy, make sure they say, 'Oh yes, Your Honour, couldn't be happier.' Because if anybody's not happy, I'll give them something to complain about afterwards . . . Oh, Lord, I'm a miserable sinner, I truly am! (*Picks up the hatbox instead of his hat.*) But I swear to you, Lord, if I get through this in one piece, I'll light you the biggest candle you've ever clapped eyes on: I'll screw every one of those swines of merchants for a hundredweight of wax. Oh God, oh God! Right, let's go, Dobchinsky! (*Makes to put on the cardboard box.*)

POLICE CHIEF. Mister Mayor, sir – that's a box, it's not a hat.

MAYOR (*flings it aside*). Dammit, so it is! And if anyone asks why the church hasn't been built, the one for the Charitable Foundation, the one we received the money for five years ago, then make sure you tell them the building was started, but it burned down. I've sent in a report about it. Only somebody might forget, some halfwit, and say it hadn't even been started. Oh, and tell Derzhimorda not to be too handy with his fists – his idea of law and order is to give everybody a black eye – innocent and guilty alike. Come on, Dobchinsky, let's go! (*Exits, then re-enters.*) And for God's sake don't let those soldiers out in their bare backsides: that garrison's a disgrace, they'll put on shirts and tunics, but they've got nothing on down below.

All exit. The Mayor's wife ANNA, *and his daughter* MARYA, *rush into the room.*

ANNA. Where are they? Where on earth have they gone? Oh, my God! (*Opens the door.*) Husband! Antosha! Anton! (*Hastily, to* MARYA.) This is all your doing, you know, it's all your

fault. Rummaging everywhere: 'I need a pin, I can't find my
scarf.' (*Runs over to the window and shouts.*) Anton! Anton, where
are you going? What? He's here? The Inspector? Has he got
a moustache? What kind of moustache has he got?

MAYOR (*off-stage*). Later, my dear, later!

ANNA. Later? What use is later? I don't want later . . . One
word, that's all: what is he? Is he a colonel? Eh? Huh! He's
gone! By heaven, I'll make you pay for this! And this one,
the whole time: 'Mama dearest, please wait for me, I've just
got to pin up my scarf, I won't be a minute.' Huh, so much
for your 'minute'! Thanks to you we've missed everything!
Vain creature: the minute she hears the Postmaster's in the
house, she's preening herself in front of the mirror – first one
side, then the other. She thinks he's after her – yes, well, he
pulls a face every time your back's turned!

MARYA. Mama, there's nothing we can do. Anyway, we'll
know all about it in a couple of hours.

ANNA. In a couple of hours! Well, thanks very much, I'm
obliged to you. Why not say a month? That'd be better still,
we'd know even more. (*Leans out of the window.*) Coo-eee!
Avdotya! Eh? What? Listen, Avdotya, have you heard anything about this newcomer? . . . You haven't? Stupid woman!
He chased you away? So what if he did, you could've asked
him anyway. You couldn't find out? Huh, your head's full of
nonsense – you've got men on the brain. What? They drove
off too quickly? Well, you could've run after the droshky,
surely? Go on, go on, do it now! Run after them, find out
where they've gone, d'you hear? Find out everything – who
this person is, what he looks like, you understand? Peep
through the keyhole, see what colour his eyes are, if they're
dark or what, then come straight back here this instant! Go
on, go on, hurry, hurry! (*She continues shouting until the curtain
falls, leaving the two women standing at the window.*)

Act Two

A small room at the inn. A bed, table, suitcase, empty bottle, boots, clothes-brush, etc. OSIP *is lying on his master's bed.*

OSIP. Dammit to hell, I'm famished! My stomach's rumbling so much it sounds like a regimental band. We'll never get home at this rate, so what d'you suggest we do, eh? That's more'n a month now, since we left Petersburg. His lordship's been chucking his money around on the road, and now he's stuck here with his tail between his legs, and he doesn't give a damn. He could've hired post-horses, he'd plenty of cash, but oh no, not him, he has to make a show of himself every place we stop. (*Mimics him.*) 'Right, Osip, go and find me a room, nothing but the best, mind, and order up the finest dinner on the menu: I can't eat any old muck, I must have the best.' I mean, it'd be a different matter if he *was* somebody, but he's only a jumped-up clerk! Yes, and he gets matey with some fly-by-night, next thing they're at the cards, and he's gambled himself into this hole! God, I'm sick to death of it! I tell you, you're better off in the country: all right, there's no social life, but you've no worries, neither – you get hold of a nice peasant woman, you can spend the rest of your days stretched out on top of the stove, eating pies. Still, you can't argue – when you come right down to it, there's no place like Petersburg. As long as you've got money, you can live like a king – them theatre places, little dancing dogs, anything you've a fancy to. And they talk so refined the whole time, you could be up there with the nobility, near as dammit. You stroll through the Shchukin market, and the traders all shout 'Your Honour!' at you. You can take the ferry-boat, and you're sitting right next to a civil servant, no less. If you fancy a bit of company, you can pop into any shop, and some army type'll tell you all the camps he's been in, or what every single star in the sky means, so you can practically see 'em, plain as day. Then some old officer's wife'll drop in, or one of them young housemaids, and by God, she'll give you such a look – whew! (*Laughs and shakes his head.*) And the manners of 'em, dammit, they're so well-bred. You won't hear a single cuss word, and everybody calls you 'sir'. And when you get fed up hoofing it, you just hop in a cab and sit yourself down like a lord – if you don't feel like paying, well, there's a back door to every house, you can skip out through it and the devil himself couldn't catch you. Only snag is, one day you're stuffing your face, the next you're practically starving, like now, for instance. And it's all his fault. I mean, what can you do with him? His old man sends him money, enough to last him a while – huh, fat chance! Next minute he's out on the town again, riding around in a cab, and every day it's: 'Get me a theatre ticket!' till by the end of the week he's sending me to the flea-market, to sell his new frock-coat. Another time he'll pawn the lot, right down to his last shirt, so's he's got nothing left but a shabby old jacket and overcoat. It's the truth, I swear to God! And nothing but the best English cloth – he'll lay out a hundred and fifty roubles on a tail-coat, then sell it at the market for twenty. And don't even mention his trousers – they'll go for practically nothing. And why's this, eh? It's because he won't give his mind to his work: yes, instead of sitting in his office, he's traipsing up and down Nevsky Prospect, or playing cards. My God, if the old master knew what was going on! I tell you, he wouldn't think twice: civil servant or no, he'd whip up your shirt tail and give you such a thrashing you wouldn't sit down for a week! You've got a decent job, so damn well do it! And the landlord's just said he won't give us nothing to eat till we pay for what we've had. And what if we can't pay, eh? (*Sighs.*) Dear God, what I wouldn't give for a bowl of cabbage soup! Honestly, I could eat a horse. There's somebody at the door – that'll be him now. (*Hurriedly removes himself from the bed.*).

KHLESTAKOV (*entering*). Here, take this. (*Hands* OSIP *his cap and cane.*) Have you been flopped out on my bed again?

OSIP. Now why would I do that? D'you think I've never seen a bed before?

KHLESTAKOV. That's a damn lie. Look at it, it's all rumpled.

OSIP. What would I want with your bed? D'you think I don't know a bed when I see one? I've got legs, I can stand. What do I need your bed for?

KHLESTAKOV (*pacing around the room*). Look in that pouch, see if there's any tobacco.

OSIP. Tobacco? That's a laugh. You smoked the last of it days ago.

KHLESTAKOV *continues pacing up and down, pursing his lips into various shapes. Finally he speaks, loudly and resolutely.*

KHLESTAKOV. Right, Osip – now you listen to me!

OSIP. Yes, sir – what is it?

KHLESTAKOV (*loudly, but not quite so resolutely*). You go down there, right?

OSIP. Down where?

KHLESTAKOV (*his voice no longer either loud or resolute, but almost pleading*). Downstairs, to the dining-room . . . And tell them . . . Tell them I'd like a bite of lunch.

OSIP. No chance. I'm not going down there.

KHLESTAKOV. What? How dare you, you ignorant lout!

OSIP. Even supposing I did go, it'd make no odds. The landlord says he's not giving us no more food.

KHLESTAKOV. Eh? What damnable cheek!

OSIP. And what's more, he says, I'm going to see the Mayor, he says – that's over two weeks now your master hasn't paid. You and that master of yours, he says, are a right pair of deadbeats, and your master's a nasty piece of work. We've seen your kind before, he says – nothing but riff-raff, the scum of the earth.

KHLESTAKOV. Yes, and you're delighted now, aren't you, you pig, telling me all this!

OSIP. We can't let just anybody come here, he says, and settle themselves in and run up a bill – we'd never get rid of them. I'm not joking, he says, I'm going to the police right now to make a complaint, to have you two flung in jail.

KHLESTAKOV. All right, that's enough, you idiot! Now, go and tell him what I said. Damned ill-mannered brute.

OSIP. Look, I'd better send the landlord up to see you himself.

KHLESTAKOV. What? What do I want with the landlord? You go and tell him.

OSIP. Honestly, sir, it's no . . .

KHLESTAKOV. All right, then, damn you! Send the landlord up. (OSIP *exits*). God, I'm absolutely ravenous! I went for a stroll, thought it might kill my appetite, but it hasn't, damn it. Yes, and if I hadn't gone on that binge in Penza, we'd have enough money to get home. That infantry captain really took me to the cleaners, he plays a marvellous game of faro, the swine. I couldn't have been sat down for more than quarter of an hour, and he skinned me alive. Even so, I was still raring to have another shot at him. Never got the chance, though. God, what a miserable dump this is. You can't even get credit at the greengrocer's. It's absolutely disgusting. (*Begins whistling a popular aria, then a folk song, finally anything that comes into his head.*) Well, looks like nobody's coming.

Enter OSIP, *with a* WAITER.

WAITER. The landlord sent me to ask what you wanted.

KHLESTAKOV. Ah, good day, my dear chap! How are you keeping?

WAITER. I'm fine, thanks be to God.

KHLESTAKOV. And how are things in the hotel line? Going well, I trust?

WAITER. Very well, thanks be to God.

KHLESTAKOV. Plenty of guests?

WAITER. Enough to be going on with.

KHLESTAKOV. Listen, my dear chap, they haven't sent up my lunch yet, so if you wouldn't mind hurrying them on a bit – I've some urgent business after lunch, you see.

WAITER. The landlord says you're not allowed any more. And he's going to make a complaint about you to the Mayor's office today.

KHLESTAKOV. What d'you mean complaint? My dear fellow, I've got to eat, you can see for yourself. Good Lord, I'm wasting away here. I'm absolutely starving, I tell you, this is serious.

WAITER. Yes, sir. He said: 'I'm giving him no more lunches, till he's paid for what he's already had.' Those were his very words, sir.

KHLESTAKOV. Well, reason with him, talk him round.

WAITER. And what am I supposed to tell him?

KHLESTAKOV. Explain to him, in all seriousness, that I need to eat. Money doesn't come into it. The man's obviously a peasant – he thinks because he can go a whole day without food, everybody else can. Well, that's news to me!

WAITER. All right, I'll tell him. (*Exits, with* OSIP.)

KHLESTAKOV. God, this is frightful, if he really won't give us anything to eat. I've never felt so hungry in my whole life. Maybe I could flog some of my clothes? A pair of trousers, say? No, I'd rather starve, than go home in anything but my best Petersburg outfit. Yes, what a pity Joachim's wouldn't hire me that carriage in Petersburg – dammit, that would've been something, rolling home in a splendid coach-and-four, driving like a demon up to some neighbour's porch, with the lights blazing, and Osip in livery perched up behind. I can just imagine them all going wild: 'Who is it? What's going on?' And then some flunkey enters (*Draws himself up and mimics a footman.*): 'Ivan Aleksandrovich Khlestakov, from St Petersburg – is Madame receiving today?' These country bumpkins don't even know what 'receiving' means. When some oaf of a landowner pays them a call, he barges straight through to the drawing-room, like a bear. And you can march right up to one of their pretty little daughters: 'Delighted to meet you, I'm sure . . . ' (*Rubs his hands together and bows.*) Ugh! (*Spits.*) Oh Lord, I feel sick, I'm so hungry.

OSIP *re-enters, followed by the* WAITER.

KHLESTAKOV. Well?

OSIP. They're bringing lunch now.

KHLESTAKOV (*claps his hands delightedly and jumps up on a chair*). Lunch! They're bringing lunch!

WAITER (*appears with plates and a napkin*). The landlord says this is the last time.

KHLESTAKOV. The landlord, the landlord, who cares? I spit on your landlord! Now, what've you got there?

WAITER. Soup and roast beef.

KHLESTAKOV. What? Two courses, is that all?

WAITER. That's the lot.

KHLESTAKOV. This is ridiculous! I won't accept it. Go back and ask him what he's playing at! This is pitiful!

WAITER. Sorry, sir, the landlord says even this is too much.

KHLESTAKOV. And what's happened to the gravy?

WAITER. There's none.

KHLESTAKOV. What d'you mean, there's none? I saw it myself, passing the kitchen, they were making gallons of gravy. And there were two little fat men in the dining-room this morning, tucking into salmon and all sorts of things.

WAITER. Well, put it this way, sir, there's gravy, and there's none.

KHLESTAKOV. What d'you mean, none?

WAITER. Just that, sir – none.

KHLESTAKOV. What, and no salmon, no fish, no rissoles?

WAITER. For the better class of customer, sir.

KHLESTAKOV. What! You ignorant creature!

WAITER. Yes, sir.

KHLESTAKOV. Listen, you disgusting pig – how come they can eat, and I can't, eh? Why can't I have the same as them, dammit? They're just passing through, same as me, aren't they?

WAITER. No, sir, they're different, it's a known fact.

KHLESTAKOV. Different in what way?

WAITER. The usual way, sir. They pay their bills, you see, that's a known fact too.

KHLESTAKOV. Right, I'm not wasting any more breath on you, you imbecile. (*Ladles out some soup and begins eating.*) Ugh! You call this soup? Dishwater in a cup. It's got no taste whatsoever, and it smells vile besides. I don't want this soup, let me have another sort.

WAITER. We'll just take it back, sir. The landlord says if you don't want it, you needn't drink it.

KHLESTAKOV (*covering his plate with his hand*). Hold on, hold on – leave it there, you idiot! You might be in the habit of treating your other guests like that, my friend, but I wouldn't advise you to try it on with me . . . (*Eats.*) Ugh, this is revolting! (*Continues eating.*) I don't think there's another person in the world that would eat this muck. Look, there's feathers floating in it instead of chicken fat. (*Cuts up some chicken pieces in the soup.*) Good Lord! You call this chicken meat? Right, let's have the roast beef! Osip, there's some soup left, you take it. (*Begins carving the roast beef.*) And what on earth's this? This isn't roast beef.

WAITER. What is it then?

KHLESTAKOV. God only knows what it is, but it isn't roast beef. They've fried up the kitchen cleaver, it's certainly not beef. (*Eats.*) Damn crooks – look what they give people to eat, eh! One mouthful of this rubbish and your jaws ache. (*Picks his teeth.*) Villains! It's like a hunk of tree-bark, that's what it's like, you can't get rid of the splinters. Two plates of this and your teeth fall out. Scoundrels! (*Wipes his mouth with a napkin.*) Well, isn't there anything else?

WAITER. No, sir.

KHLESTAKOV. Rabble! Scum! If there'd even been a spot of gravy, or a pie. Layabouts – that's all you're good for, robbing innocent travellers!

The WAITER *and* OSIP *clear the table and remove the dishes.*

Honest to God, it's as if I'd eaten nothing. Just enough to whet my appetite. If I'd even a few coppers, I'd send out to the market for a bun.

OSIP (*re-enters*). The Mayor's arrived! He's downstairs now, asking all kinds of questions about you.

KHLESTAKOV (*alarmed*). I don't believe it! That swine of a landlord must've sent his complaint in already! Oh, my God, what if they really do drag me off to jail? Oh well, I suppose if they treat me like a gentleman, I might . . . No, no, I can't! There are officers and all sorts traipsing around the town, and it's as if it's happened on purpose, I've been putting on airs, and giving some merchant's daughter the eye . . . No, I can't face it . . . I mean, really, how dare he do this to me! Who does he think I am, some wretched tradesman or shopkeeper? (*Draws himself up to his full height.*) I'll tell him to his face, by God: 'Just who do you think you are, eh?'

Someone turns the door-handle, KHLESTAKOV goes pale, and cringes. The MAYOR enters, followed by DOBCHINSKY, and stops in his tracks. KHLESTAKOV and the MAYOR stare at each other, both goggle-eyed with fright, for a few moments. The MAYOR recovers his composure slightly, and comes to attention.

MAYOR. Sir, I have the honour to wish you good day.

KHLESTAKOV (*bows*). Not at all, the honour's mine . . .

MAYOR. And pardon my intrusion, sir, but . . .

KHLESTAKOV. Don't mention it.

MAYOR. You see, sir, it's my duty, as Mayor of this town, to ensure that visitors, and people of rank, are in no way inconvenienced . . .

KHLESTAKOV (*stammering at first, but by the end of his speech, almost shouting*). Well, what can I do? It's not my fault . . . I'll pay the bill, honestly . . . I'll have some money sent from home. (BOBCHINSKY *peeps round the door.*) Actually, the landlord's more to blame than me. Roast beef he dishes up, and it's as hard as a lump of wood. And as for the soup – God only knows what he slops into that, I had to chuck it out of the window. He's been starving me to death for days on end. And his tea's most peculiar – it smells more like fish than tea! So why should I be put in . . . Oh, honestly, I don't believe this!

MAYOR (*meekly*). Forgive me, sir, it isn't my fault. The beef I see in our market is always top-quality. The traders bring it down from Archangel, they're sober, well-behaved people, sir. I've no idea where he gets his from. But if things here aren't to your liking, sir, well . . . Perhaps you'll allow me to escort you to another apartment.

KHLESTAKOV. No, not on your life! I know what you mean
by another apartment – you mean jail! What right have you,
eh? How dare you, sir? Dammit, I'm in Government service!
I'm from St Petersburg! (*Plucking up courage.*) I'm . . . I'm . . .
I'm . . .

MAYOR (*aside*). Oh, my God, he's furious! He knows
everything, those swines of merchants have spilled the beans!

KHLESTAKOV (*blustering*). Yes, you can bring a whole
regiment here if you like, I'm not moving! I shall go straight
to the Minister! (*Pounds his fist on the table.*) How dare you, sir!
How dare you!

MAYOR (*standing at attention, trembling all over*). Oh God, have
mercy, sir, don't ruin me! My poor wife, my dear little
children . . . please, don't destroy my life!

KHLESTAKOV. No, I won't have it! This is ridiculous, what's
that to do with me? Just because you've a wife and kids, I'm
supposed to go to jail – that's priceless!

BOBCHINSKY *peeps round the door, and withdraws in alarm.*

No, sir – I thank you most humbly, but I won't have it!

MAYOR. It was inexperience, honest to God, sir, that's all it
was – pure inexperience. That, and insufficient funds . . .
You know yourself, sir: a Government salary'll hardly keep
you in tea and sugar, and if I did take the odd bribe, well, it
was the merest trifle – something for the table, or a bit of
cloth for a suit. All that stuff about the sergeant's widow, the
one that keeps the shop, the one I'm supposed to have had
flogged, that's all lies, sir, I swear to God, that's slander, sir,
dreamed up by my enemies. Oh yes, there's people in this
town just itching to make an attempt on my life!

KHLESTAKOV. So what? I've nothing to do with them.
(*Pensively.*) Look, I've no idea why you're going on about
assassins, or this sergeant's widow . . . A sergeant's widow's
one thing, but if you think you can flog me, that's a different
kettle of fish entirely . . . Damn cheek of the man! Anyway,

I will pay, I'll pay my bill, I just don't have the money on me right now. That's why I'm stuck in this hole, because I don't have a single kopeck.

MAYOR (*aside*). Oh, this is a crafty devil! You can see what he's after, but what a smokescreen he puts up, you can barely figure him out. You don't know which way to take him. Well, I'll put him to the test. *Che sera, sera*, as they say – I'll give it a try. (*Aloud.*) Actually, if you really are short of cash, or anything else for that matter, I'm only too ready to be of service. After all, it's my duty to assist our visitors.

KHLESTAKOV. Yes, do, lend me some money! I'll settle up with the landlord right now. All I need is a couple of hundred roubles, maybe even less.

MAYOR (*produces a wad of banknotes*). There we are, sir, two hundred roubles exactly – don't even bother to count it.

KHLESTAKOV (*takes the money*). Well, thanks most awfully. I'll return this to you the minute I get back to my estate. I don't put off things like that. Yes, I can see you're a gentleman, sir. That puts an entirely different light on the matter.

MAYOR (*aside*). Thank God for that! He's taken the money. Everything'll go smoothly now, I think. And that was four hundred I slipped him, not two.

KHLESTAKOV. Hey, Osip! (OSIP *enters.*) Call that waiter back up here! (*To the* MAYOR *and* DOBCHINSKY.) Heavens, why are you standing? Gentlemen, please be seated. (*To* DOBCHINSKY.) Sit down, please, I beg you.

MAYOR. Not at all, we're happy to stand.

KHLESTAKOV. Sit down, do, please. I can see perfectly well now how open and hospitable you are, but I must confess, I thought you'd actually come to put me . . . (*To* DOBCHINSKY.) Do please sit down!

The MAYOR *and* DOBCHINSKY *sit.* BOBCHINSKY *peeps round the door, straining to listen.*

MAYOR (*aside*). Might as well go the whole hog. Obviously wants to preserve his incognito. That's fine, we'll play dumb too: we'll pretend we haven't a clue who he is. (*Aloud.*) As a matter of fact, we were just passing on business, myself and Dobchinsky here – he's a local landowner – and we purposely dropped into the inn here, to check that our visitors were being well looked after, because I'm not like some other mayors, who couldn't care less. No, sir, not just out of duty, but pure Christian love for my fellow-man, I want every mortal soul to have a decent welcome here – and now, as luck would have it, by way of reward, I have the pleasure of making your acquaintance.

KHLESTAKOV. And I yours, sir. I must confess that if you hadn't turned up, I might've been stuck here for a very long time. I had absolutely no idea how I was going to pay.

MAYOR (*aside*). Yes, tell us another one! (*Aloud.*) Sir, if I may make so bold – may I ask in which direction you might be heading?

KHLESTAKOV. I'm travelling to Saratov, to my country estate.

MAYOR (*aside, with an ironic expression*). Saratov, indeed! And he says it without a blush! Oh yes, this fellow'll take some watching. (*Aloud.*) Well, that's a noble undertaking, sir – travel, I mean. Although they do say it has its pros and cons. It can be a bit of a nuisance, changing horses and the like, but then again, it does broaden the mind. I take it, sir, that you're travelling for your own pleasure, in the main?

KHLESTAKOV. No, my father's demanding to see me. The old boy's a bit miffed because I haven't earned myself a promotion yet in Petersburg. He thinks you only have to turn up, and they give you the Order of St Vladimir to stick in your buttonhole. I'd like to see *him* grinding away in some office.

MAYOR (*aside*). By God, he can't half spin a yarn, this one! Even dragging in his old dad! (*Aloud.*) Tell me, sir, do you intend a long stay?

KHLESTAKOV. I honestly don't know. My father's so damned obstinate, he's like a lump of wood, the silly old fool. I'll tell him straight out: you can say what you like, but I can't live anywhere else but Petersburg. Good heavens, am I supposed to waste away among a bunch of peasants? People want different things out of life nowadays, and my spirit craves enlightenment.

MAYOR (*aside*). Fantastic! What a memory! One lie after another, and he never puts a foot wrong. And he seems such a miserable, insignificant creature – you could squash him with your fingernail. Well, sir, just you wait – I'll catch you out soon enough. I think I'll make you tell us a bit more. (*Aloud.*) Yes, you're absolutely right, sir. After all, what can one do at the back of beyond? Take this very town: the sleepless nights you spend, agonizing over your country, slaving away, but as for just reward – well, who knows when that'll come? (*Casts his eye over the room.*) Looks a bit damp, this place, don't you think?

KHLESTAKOV. It's a filthy hole – bug-ridden, I've never seen anything like it. Honestly, they bite worse than dogs.

MAYOR. Good heavens! A distinguished visitor like yourself, and what's he got to put up with? Good-for-nothing bedbugs, that should never've seen the light of day! I suppose this room's dark as well?

KHLESTAKOV. Pitch dark, yes. Seems the landlord's lost the habit of dishing out candles. So, now and again when I feel like doing something – reading, say, or writing myself, when the fancy takes me – I can't, it's too damned dark.

MAYOR. Oh dear, I hardly dare ask . . . no, I can't, I'm not worthy.

KHLESTAKOV. Worthy of what?

MAYOR. No, it's too presumptuous of me.

KHLESTAKOV. What are you talking about?

MAYOR. Sir, if I may be so bold . . . There's a first-class room
you can have in my house, well-lit, quiet . . . No, no, it
would be too great an honour, I'm only too well aware . . .
Please, don't be angry, sir – God knows, it's a simple heart
that offers . . .

KHLESTAKOV. On the contrary, sir, I accept with pleasure.
I'll be far better off in a private house, than in this miserable
dump.

MAYOR. Oh, I'd be absolutely delighted! And my dear wife
too! That's just the way I am, sir, I'm a hospitable man,
always have been, especially when it's a enlightened person
like yourself. And don't think I'm saying this out of flattery.
No, sir, that's a vice I don't possess. I'm expressing my
feelings, sir, out of a full heart.

KHLESTAKOV. Well, thank you very much. I can't abide
two-faced people either, I must say. I'm greatly taken by
your frankness and generosity, and I'll freely confess to you,
I demand no more from this life than devotion and respect.
Yes, show me respect and devotion, that's all I ask.

Enter the WAITER, *accompanied by* OSIP. BOBCHINSKY
peeps round the door.

WAITER. Did you wish anything, sir?

KHLESTAKOV. Yes, let's have the bill.

WAITER. Sir, I gave you another bill just now.

KHLESTAKOV. I can't keep track of all your stupid bills. How
much is it?

WAITER. Well, you ordered the set dinner the first day, then
just a starter of smoked salmon the next day, and after that
you had everything put on the slate.

KHLESTAKOV. Idiot! Don't start totting it all up again, just
tell me how much.

MAYOR. There's no need to concern yourself, dear sir – he can wait. (*To the* WAITER.) Go on, clear off – I'll settle up later . . .

KHLESTAKOV. Really? That's very decent of you.

He puts away his wad of notes, and the WAITER *exits.* BOBCHINSKY *again peeps round the door.*

MAYOR. Now, sir, if you'd care to inspect some of our civic buildings – charitable institutions, workhouses and such like . . .

KHLESTAKOV. What on earth for?

MAYOR. Well, you'd see how we run things here . . . how we do business . . .

KHLESTAKOV. Well, why not? I'd be delighted.

BOBCHINSKY sticks his head round the door.

MAYOR. Then if you wish, we can go on from there to the district school, to see our methods of instruction in the various subjects.

KHLESTAKOV. Yes, by all means.

MAYOR. After that, if you like, we can visit the town jail and inspect the cells – have a look at how treat our criminals.

KHLESTAKOV. Cells? Why the devil should I want to see them? I'd much rather we inspected your workhouses.

MAYOR. Whatever you say, sir. Now, how do you intend to proceed? Will you take your own carriage, or ride with myself in the droshky?

KHLESTAKOV. I think I'd better come with you in the droshky.

MAYOR (*to* DOBCHINSKY). Right, Dobchinsky, that's your seat gone.

DOBCHINSKY. Doesn't matter, I'll manage.

MAYOR (*to* DOBCHINSKY, *sotto voce*). Listen, Dobchinsky, run like the wind – as fast as your legs'll carry you, d'you hear? – and take these two notes, one to Zemlyanika at the workhouse, and the other one to my wife. (*To* KHLESTAKOV.) My dear sir, I wonder if I might crave your indulgence a moment, while I pen a line or two in your presence to my dear wife, to bid her prepare for the arrival of our honoured guest?

KHLESTAKOV. Really, must you? . . . Well, there is ink here, but I don't know about paper . . . Unless you write on this bill?

MAYOR. Yes, that'll do. (*Writes, and talks to himself at the same time.*) Well, now, let's see how things go after a decent lunch, and a nice pot-bellied bottle of wine! He can have some of our local Madeira – unpretentious, but it'll bring down an elephant. If I could just find out what he's up to, and how far we have to watch out for him.

He finishes writing, and hands the notes to DOBCHINSKY, *who makes for the door. At that moment, the door flies off its hinges and crashes onto the stage, bringing with it* BOBCHINSKY, *who has been eavesdropping behind it. General uproar, as* BOBCHINSKY *picks himself up from the floor.*

KHLESTAKOV. Good Lord, you haven't damaged anything, I hope?

BOBCHINSKY. Oh no, sir, no – nothing to get excited about, just a little bump on the nose. I'll run over to Dr Gibner's – he does a very good plaster, that should do the trick.

MAYOR (*looks daggers at* BOBCHINSKY, *then to* KHLESTAKOV). It's a mere trifle, sir. Now, if you'd be so kind as to accompany me, I'll tell your man to bring on your luggage. (*To* OSIP.) Right, my good man, you're to convey everything to me, at the Mayor's house, anybody'll point it out to you. (*To* KHLESTAKOV.) No, no, sir, after you. (*Waves* KHLESTAKOV *ahead, and follows him out, but turns round to rebuke* BOBCHINSKY.) Trust you! You couldn't have found somewhere else to collapse? Stretched out on the floor like God knows what! (*Exits, followed by* BOBCHINSKY.)

Curtain.

Act Three

The same room as in Act One. The Mayor's wife ANNA *and daughter* MARYA *are standing at the window in the same positions.*

ANNA. Now look, that's a whole hour we've waited, and all because of your silly airs and graces: she's dressed to perfection, but no, she has to go rummaging some more . . . I shouldn't even have listened to her. Oh, it makes me so angry! And there's not a soul to be seen, of course. You'd think they'd all died.

MARYA. Honestly, mama, we'll know everything in a minute. Avdotya's bound to appear soon. (*Peers through the window and suddenly shrieks.*) Oh, mama, mama! There's someone coming, look, at the end of the street!

ANNA. Coming where? You see things, that's your trouble. Wait, there *is* somebody – who is it? Quite short . . . in a frock-coat . . . Who is it? Oh, this is so infuriating! Who on earth can it be?

MARYA: Mama, it's Dobchinsky.

ANNA: Dobchinsky my foot – you're imagining things as usual. That's never Dobchinsky. (*Waves her handkerchief at him.*) Hey! You, sir! Come here, quickly!

MARYA. Mama, it is Dobchinsky, honestly.

ANNA. You see? You're doing it again, just to be contrary. I'm telling you it's *not* Dobchinsky.

MARYA. What? Mama, what d'you mean? Look, you can see it's Dobchinsky.

ANNA. All right, it is Dobchinsky – I can see him now, what

are you arguing about? (*Shouts out of the window.*) Oh, hurry up for heaven's sake! You're going too slowly. Come on, where are they? Eh? No, no, you can tell me from there, that'll do. What? Is he very strict? Eh? What about the Mayor, what about my husband? (*Steps back from the window, annoyed.*) The man's a fool! He won't tell us a thing till he's in the room!

DOBCHINSKY *enters.*

Well, you're a fine one — you should be ashamed of yourself. I was relying on you especially, you're supposed to be a sensible chap, but no, they all suddenly run off, and you follow them! And I still can't get a word of sense out of anybody! Aren't you ashamed of yourself? I was godmother to your little Vanya and Liza, and this is how you treat me!

DOBCHINSKY. Anna Andreevna, I swear to God, I've run so fast to pay my respects to you here, I can scarcely draw breath. My respects to you too, Marya Antonovna.

MARYA. Good morning, Pyotr Ivanovich.

ANNA. Well? Go on — tell us what's happening!

DOBCHINSKY. Ma'am, the Mayor's sent you a note.

ANNA. Well, who is this fellow? Is he a general?

DOBCHINSKY. No, not a general, but not far short. He's so well educated, really impressive manners.

ANNA. Aha! Then it must be the man in my husband's letter.

DOBCHINSKY. The very same. And I was the first to discover him, along with Bobchinsky.

ANNA. Well, get on with it — tell us what's happening!

DOBCHINSKY: Everything's going smoothly, thank goodness. He was a bit hard on the Mayor to start with — oh yes, ma'am, he got quite angry, said everything in the inn was terrible, but he wouldn't come here either, and said he wasn't going to jail on the Mayor's account. Then after a bit, when he realised it wasn't the Mayor's fault, and they'd had a little chat, well, he changed his mind right there and then, and it all went off swimmingly, thank goodness. They've gone to inspect the workhouse and the hospital now . . . I'll tell you straight, ma'am, the Mayor thought there might've been some secret report on him, and that gave me a bit of a scare too.

ANNA. What've you got to worry about? You're not even in the service.

DOBCHINSKY. Yes, I know, but when these bigwigs start talking, it does give you a turn.

ANNA. Oh, don't be ridiculous. That's enough nonsense — tell us what he looks like. Is he young or old?

DOBCHINSKY. Young, quite young — about twenty-three — but he talks just like an old man: 'Very well', he says, 'I shall see this, and that . . . ' (*Airily waving his hand.*) Absolutely the last word. 'I like to do a bit of writing and reading,' he says, 'but I'm prevented in this room,' he says, 'because it's a trifle dark.'

ANNA. Yes, but what does he look like: is he dark or fair?

DOBCHINSKY. No, he's more auburn, and so quick and sharp-eyed, he's like a fox, it makes you feel quite nervous.

ANNA. Anyway, what does he say in this note? (*Reads.*) 'I hasten to inform you, my dearest, that my situation appeared grave in the extreme, but trusting in God's mercy, for two pickled cucumbers, extra, and a half-portion of caviar, one rouble twenty-five kopecks . . . ' (*Stops.*) I can't make this out: what's he talking about, pickled cucumbers and caviar?

DOBCHINBSKY. Ah, that's because the Mayor had to write it in a hurry, on scrap paper: that must be his bill.

ANNA. So it is. (*Carries on reading.*) 'But trusting in God's mercy, everything will turn out well, I think. Prepare a room quickly for our distinguished guest: the one with the yellow wallpaper; don't concern yourself about another place at dinner, we'll have a bite at the workhouse with Zemlyanika, but do order some more wine; tell the merchant Abdulin to send nothing but the best, otherwise I'll turn his whole cellar inside out. I kiss your hand, my dearest – yours ever, Anton . . . ' Oh, my God! We'd better get busy! Right, who's out there? Mishka!

DOBCHINSKY (*Runs to the door and shouts*). Mishka! Mishka! Mishka!

MISHKA *enters*.

ANNA. Listen – run over to Abdulin's shop . . . no, wait a minute, I'll make out a list. (*Sits down at the table and begins writing.*) Give this list to Sidor the coachman, tell him to run with it to Abdulin's and bring back the wine. Then tidy up the spare room for our guest, and make sure you do it right. Put a bed in there, a wash-basin and the like. (MISHKA *exits.*)

DOBCHINSKY. I'd better run along now, dear lady, see how he's getting on with the inspection.

ANNA. Go on, go on – nobody's stopping you!

DOBCHINSKY *exits*.

Now, Masha my dear, we'll need to make ourselves presentable. He's from St Petersburg , God forbid he should find something to laugh at. You'd better wear your pale blue dress with the little flounces.

MARYA. Ugh! Mama, not the pale blue! I absolutely hate it, the Judge's wife wears pale blue, and so does Zemlyanika's daughter. No, I'd rather wear the one with the flowers.

ANNA. Flowers! Honestly, you'd say anything, just to be awkward. The blue'll be much better, it'll go with my pale yellow, my little straw-coloured dress, the one I'm so fond of.

MARYA. Mama, yellow doesn't suit you at all!

ANNA. Yellow doesn't suit me?

MARYA. No, it doesn't, I don't care what you say. You need really dark eyes for that colour.

ANNA. What a cheek! Are you telling me I don't have dark eyes? They're extremely dark. Really, what nonsense you talk. If they're not dark, then how is it, whenever we're telling fortunes, I'm always the Queen of Clubs?

MARYA. Mama, the Queen of Hearts is more your style.

ANNA. That's rubbish, absolute rubbish! I've never been the Queen of Hearts! (*Storms out, followed by* MARYA, *still talking off-stage.*) Honestly, the stuff she comes out with! Queen of Hearts! God knows what she'll think up next!

As they exit, the doors open and MISHKA *flings out some trash.* OSIP *enters by another door, carrying a trunk on his head.*

OSIP. So where's this to go?

MISHKA. In here, grandad, in here.

OSIP. Hang on till I get my breath back. God, what a miserable life! This weighs twice as much on an empty stomach, you know.

MISHKA. So tell us, grandad, will the general be here soon?

OSIP. Eh? What general?

MISHKA. Your master, of course.

OSIP. My master? What gives you that idea?

MISHKA. D'you mean he's not a general?

OSIP. Oh, he's a general all right, and then some.

MISHKA. So what's that? Does that mean he's higher or lower than a real general?

OSIP. Higher.

MISHKA. Really? So that's why they're kicking up such a fuss.

OSIP. Listen, son – I can see you're a smart lad. Do us a favour and get us a bite to eat.

MISHKA. Sorry, grandad, there's nothing ready for you yet. I mean, you won't want just any old grub, but as soon as your master sits down to his dinner, they'll dish up the exact same to you.

OSIP. Well, what do you call any old grub?

MISHKA. Cabbage soup, porridge, pies . . .

OSIP. Right, let's have them – cabbage soup, porridge, and pies. Don't you worry, I'll eat the lot. Come on, give us a hand with this trunk. Is there another way out of here?

MISHKA. Yes, there is.

They carry out the trunk into a side room. The double doors are opened by two CONSTABLES. *Enter* KHLESTAKOV, *followed by the* MAYOR, *the* CHARITIES WARDEN, *the* SUPERINTEN-DENT OF SCHOOLS, DOBCHINSKY *and* BOBCHINSKY, *with a plaster on his nose. The* MAYOR *points to a scrap of paper on the floor, and the* CONSTABLES *rush to pick it up, colliding in their haste.*

KHLESTAKOV. Yes, very fine institutions. I do like the way you show visitors round the whole town. No-one ever showed me anything in other places.

MAYOR. Well, if I may be so bold, sir – that's because the administrators and officials in other towns are more concerned with – put it this way – their own advantage. Here, on the other hand, I may say we have no thought but how to earn the good opinion of our superiors, by diligently observing the proprieties.

KHLESTAKOV. Lunch was rather decent, I thought. I'm quite full up. Do you eat like that every day?

MAYOR. Laid on specially for our honoured guest, sir.

KHLESTAKOV. Yes, I do enjoy eating. After all, what's life for, but to graze among pleasure's blooms? What was that fish called?

WARDEN (*Scurrying up*). Labberdaan, sir – it's a kind of salt cod.

KHLESTAKOV. It was very tasty. Where did we have lunch again? The hospital, was it?

WARDEN. That's correct, sir – the charity hospital.

KHLESTAKOV. Ah yes, I remember seeing some beds. So, have your patients all recovered? There didn't seem that many.

WARDEN. There's about a dozen left, sir, the rest have all recovered. It's the system we operate here. Since I took over the running of the place – you'll perhaps find this incredible, sir – they've been recovering like flies. A patient's scarcely set foot in the hospital before he's cured, and not through expensive medicines either, but good old-fashioned discipline.

MAYOR. If I may make so bold, sir – the duties of the chief executive – now, they're fiendishly difficult. I've so much on my plate, keeping the streets clean, repairs, putting things to rights . . . I tell you, sir, it'd bamboozle the cleverest of men, but thanks be to God, it's all running smoothly. Other mayors, of course, would be looking after their own interests, but believe it or not, sir, last thing at night, as I go to bed, I'm still thinking: 'Lord God above, how can I fix it so that the authorities will see how diligent I am, and be happy with me?' Whether I'm rewarded or not, well, that's up to them, but at least I'll be at peace in my heart. After all, if the town's in good order, the streets swept, the prisoners looked after, drunks kept to a minimum, what more can one ask, eh? No no, sir, it's not honours I'm after. They have their attractions, of course, but virtue is its own reward.

WARDEN (*aside*). That's some yarn he's spinning, the idle layabout. Talk about the gift of the gab!

KHLESTAKOV. Yes, that's very true. Actually, I do a bit of serious thinking myself now and again. Sometimes in prose, but I occasionally dash off the odd verse.

BOBCHINSKY (*to* DOBCHINSKY). That's the one, Pyotr Ivanovich, we're absolutely right. The way he expresses things . . . he's obviously had a good education.

KHLESTAKOV. Tell me, sirs, do you by any chance have any sort of amusements, a club, say, where one might have a game of cards?

MAYOR (*aside*). Oho, my fine fellow, now I see what you're driving at! (*Aloud.*) Heaven forfend, sir! We haven't any clubs of that sort, wouldn't hear of them. I've never picked up a card in my life, wouldn't even know how to play. I can't bear to look at them, and if by chance I do catch sight of some King of Diamonds or whatever, I feel so disgusted I could just about spit. Matter of fact, I did once build a house of cards, to amuse the children, and afterwards I had nightmares about the wretched things. No, God forbid, sir, I don't know how people can waste precious time on them.

SUPERINTENDENT (*aside*). Yes, the swine only took me for a hundred roubles last night!

MAYOR. No no, I'd rather devote my time to serving the State.

KHLESTAKOV. Well, I think you're going a bit far. It all depends on your point of view, doesn't it. For instance, if you're the sort of chap who sticks, when you should treble your stake, well, of course . . . No, don't say that, the odd game of cards can be very tempting.

Enter ANNA *and* MARYA.

MAYOR. Sir, allow me to present my family: my wife and daughter.

KHLESTAKOV (*bowing*). Madam, I'm delighted to have the particular pleasure of meeting you.

ANNA. And it's even more of a pleasure for us to meet such a distinguished personage.

KHLESTAKOV (*striking a pose*). On the contrary, ma'am – the pleasure is entirely mine.

ANNA. Oh, sir, how can you? You're only saying that out of politeness. Please, do sit down.

KHLESTAKOV. Just to stand near you is happiness enough, dear lady. However, if you absolutely insist, I shall sit down. (*Sits.*) There – I'm sitting beside you, my happiness is complete.

ANNA. Heavens, sir, I can't believe you mean me . . . I'm sure you must find travelling in the country most disagreeable after St Petersburg.

KHLESTAKOV. Oh, disagreeable in the extreme. One gets accustomed to the *beau monde, comprenez-vous*, and then to find oneself on the road: filthy taverns, a veritable fog of ignorance . . . I will confess to you, ma'am, that if it hadn't been for this *bonne chance* . . . (*Looks round at* ANNA, *and strikes a pose.*) which has so richly compensated me for all that . . .

ANNA. Oh, sir, how dreadful it must've been for you!

KHLESTAKOV. Anyway, dear lady, at this moment, I am extremely happy.

ANNA. Goodness, so many compliments. I don't deserve them.

KHLESTAKOV. And why in heaven's name not? Of *course* you deserve them, dear lady.

ANNA. But I live in the country . . .

KHLESTAKOV. Ah, but the country has charms of its own – gentle hillocks, shady rills . . . Though naturally it can't compare with St Petersburg. Oh, Petersburg! Now *there*'s a life for you. No doubt you think I'm a mere pen-pusher, but let me tell you, the head of department and I are like *that!* (*Crosses his fingers.*) Yes, he claps me on the shoulder, he says: 'Drop in for dinner, old chap!' I pop into the office for a couple of minutes, just to say: 'Right, do this, do that!' And the copy clerk, miserable rat of a fellow, picks up his pen,

starts scratching away. Actually they wanted to make me a
collegiate assessor, but I thought, well, what's the point? And
the porter comes flying downstairs after me with his brush:
'Sir, sir, he says, please let me give your boots a polish!'
(*To the* MAYOR.) Good heavens, gentlemen, why are you
standing? Sit down, please.

The MAYOR, WARDEN, *and* SUPERINTENDENT *all
speak together.*

MAYOR. Sir, we know our place – we don't mind standing.

WARDEN. We're happy to stand.

SUPERINTENDENT. Don't concern yourself, sir!

KHLESTAKOV. Gentlemen, don't stand on ceremony – sit
down, please. (*They do so.*) I can't abide all that stuff. As a
matter of fact, I even try to slip into places incognito. But it's
quite impossible, you simply can't hide. I've only got to step
outside the door, and it's: 'Look, there he goes, it's Ivan
Aleksandrovich!' On one occasion I was even mistaken for
the Commander-in-Chief: the soldiers tumbled out of the
guard-house and presented arms. And afterwards their officer
– who's a friend of mine in fact – told me: 'You know, we
really did take you for the Commander-in-Chief, old boy.'

ANNA. Fancy that!

KHLESTAKOV. And I know all the best-looking actresses. I
write the odd vaudeville sketch, you see, and I'm pretty well
in with the literary types. Yes, Pushkin and I are like that.
(*Crosses his fingers.*) I often say to him: 'Well, Pushkin, old
chap, how are things?' And he'll say: 'Oh, so-so, old boy,
can't complain . . . ' Yes, he's a real character.

ANNA. So you're a writer too? It must be wonderful to be so
talented! I suppose you get things into the papers?

KHLESTAKOV. I do, as a matter of fact. Actually, I've written
lots of things: 'Marriage of Figaro', 'Robert le Diable',
'Norma' – I can't even remember their names. It came about

by chance, really – I couldn't be bothered writing, but the theatre management kept after me: 'Please, please, old boy, write something for us.' So, I think to myself: 'Well, why not? I'll give it a try.' And that very same night, would you believe, I wrote the whole thing – left 'em all speechless. Yes, I have a quite extraordinary facility of thought. All that stuff you read under the name of Baron Brambeus – 'Frigate of Hope', 'Moscow Telegraph' and so forth – that's mine, you know.

ANNA. You're honestly Baron Brambeus?

KHLESTAKOV. Oh yes, I sort out all their articles. Smirdin gives me forty thousand for that.

ANNA. Then 'Yuri Miloslavsky' must be your handiwork as well.

KHLESTAKOV. Yes, that's mine.

ANNA. I knew it, I knew it.

MARYA. Actually, mama, it says on the cover it was written by a Mr Zagoskin.

ANNA. You see? I knew you'd start an argument, I knew you would.

KHLESTAKOV. No no, she's quite right. There is one by Zagoskin, but there's another 'Yuri Miloslavsky', and that one's mine.

ANNA. Oh well, it must be yours I've read. It's so beautifully written.

KHLESTAKOV. Yes, I must admit I simply live for literature. I have the very first house in St Petersburg, everybody knows it: Khlestakov's house. (*Turns to address them all.*) Gentlemen, if you're ever in St Petersburg, please, please, do me the kindness of calling on me. I give balls too, you know.

ANNA. Oh, I can just imagine those balls, they must be magnificent, and so tasteful!

KHLESTAKOV. They're beyond words, ma'am. Melons on
the table, for instance – seven hundred roubles apiece. Soup
shipped in direct from Paris, still in the pot – you lift the lid,
and the aroma, well, it's just out of this world! And I'm out
at a ball every evening. We get up our own little whist party:
the Foreign Minister, the French Ambassador, the English
and German Ambassadors, and myself. You can practically
kill yourself playing cards, you wouldn't believe it. I mean,
you run up the stairs to the fourth floor, and you can just
about manage to say to the cook: 'Here, Mavra, old girl, take
my coat . . . ' What am I talking about? I've forgotten I live
on the first floor! My staircase alone must be worth, oh . . .
And you should see my waiting-room, even before I'm up,
it's a sight to behold – counts and princes, all buzzing
around, bumping into each other, like a swarm of bees, that's
all you hear – buzz-buzz-buzz . . . Now and again the
Minister himself . . . (*The* MAYOR *and the others rise timidly
from their chairs.*) I even get parcels addressed to 'Your
Excellency'. I was in charge of the department once too – an
odd business, the Director went off somewhere, Lord knows
where, and of course, there was a lot of talk about who
should take over. Generals and everything volunteered for
the job, but when it came to the bit, well, they just weren't
up to it. It's not as easy as it looks, by God, it's not! Anyway,
there was nothing else for it, they could see that, they had to
send for me. So next minute the streets were full of
messengers, running all over the place – thirty-five thousand
messengers, would you believe! 'What's the problem?' I ask.
'Ivan Aleksandrovich, please, you must take over the
department!' Well, I was somewhat nonplussed, I can tell
you, standing there in my dressing-gown. I'd have turned it
down, but I thought, no, this'll reach His Majesty's ears, and
go on my service record besides . . . 'Very well, gentlemen,
I said, I accept the post, I'll take it on, I said, only I won't
stand for any nonsense, d'you hear? I've got my eye on you
lot, so watch out!' And that's just what happened, by God,
every time I walked through that department, you'd have
thought an earthquake had struck, they were shaking in their

shoes, believe me. (*The* MAYOR *and the others are trembling with fear.* KHLESTAKOV *is warming to his task.*) I don't stand for any funny business, no, not me. I put the fear of God into that lot. Even His Majesty's Privy Council's frightened of me. And so they should be. That's the kind of man I am. I don't care who they are, I'll say it to anybody: 'I'm my own man, sir, so there!' I'm here, there and everywhere. I drive to the palace every day. And tomorrow, would you believe, they're making me a Field-Marshal . . .

In his excitement, KHLESTAKOV *slips and almost crashes to the floor, but the officials respectfully keep him upright. The* MAYOR *approaches, trembling from head to foot, scarcely able to speak.*

MAYOR. B-b-but . . . Y-y-you . . . y-y-you . . .

KHLESTAKOV (*testily*). Yes, what is it?

MAYOR. B-b-but . . . Y-y-you . . . y-y-you . . .

KHLESTAKOV (*in the same tone*). I can't make out a word. You're gibbering, sir.

MAYOR. Y-y-you . . . your Youness, your Highness, please, won't you rest a while? Your room's ready, there's everything you need.

KHLESTAKOV. Rest? Rubbish! Oh, all right then, I wouldn't mind a lie-down. Yes, you do a decent lunch, gentlemen . . . Not bad, not bad at all. (*Theatrically.*) Labardaan! Labardaan! (*Exits to a side room, followed by the* MAYOR.)

BOBCHINSKY (*to* DOBCHINSKY). Well, Dobchinsky, that's quite a man, eh? That's what you call a man! In all my born days I've never once been in the presence of such an important personage – I tell you, I just about died of fright. What d'you think, Dobchinsky? Where would you place him as regards rank?

DOBCHINSKY. Oh, he can't be far off a general.

BOBCHINSKY. What? A general isn't fit to tie his shoe-laces! Or if he is a general, he must be the Generalissimo himself.

Didn't you hear the way he cracked down on the Privy Council? We'd better hurry and tell all this to the Judge and Korobkin. Goodbye, Anna Andreevna.

DOBCHINSKY. Goodbye, dear lady. (*They exit.*)

WARDEN (*to* SUPERINTENDENT). Oh Lord, I'm scared stiff, absolutely petrified. And I don't understand why. We're not even in uniform. And what's going to happen when he wakes up and fires off that report to St Petersburg? (*Exits, deep in thought, followed by the* SUPERINTENDENT.) Goodbye, ma'am.

ANNA. Oh, what a charming man!

MARYA. An absolute darling!

ANNA. But with such a refined manner. You can tell instantly he's a Petersburg type. His bearing, the way he holds himself . . . Oh, it's just wonderful! I absolutely adore young men like that. I could almost swoon. And he obviously took a fancy to me, I noticed that much. He couldn't keep his eyes off me.

MARYA. Oh, mama, it was *me* he was looking at!

ANNA. Oh, for heaven's sake, spare me your nonsense. I've just about had enough for one day.

MARYA. No, mama, honestly!

ANNA. God preserve us, you'd say anything to be contrary! That's enough, d'you hear? What would he want to look at you for? Eh? What earthly reason could he have for looking at you?

MARYA. It's the truth, mama, he was watching me the whole time. When he started talking about literature, he glanced over at me, and afterwards when he was telling us about playing whist with the ambassadors, he looked at me then too.

ANNA. Well, he maybe threw you the odd glance, but just once, if at all. 'Oh yes,' he'll have said to himself, 'I suppose I'd better look at her now.'

MAYOR (*entering on tiptoe*). Sshhh . . . sshhh!

ANNA. What is it?

MAYOR. I wish I hadn't got him drunk. Suppose even half of what he said is true? (*Thinks.*) And why shouldn't it be true, eh? When a man's half-sozzled like that he gives everything away. *In vino veritas*, as they say. Of course, he'll have embroidered a bit, but if you can't do that these days, you might as well shut up. Good heavens, he plays cards with Ministers and drives to the Palace . . . Honestly, the more you think about it . . . God only knows what this is doing to my head, it's as if I'm perched on top of a steeple, or waiting to be hanged.

ANNA. Well, I didn't feel in the least intimidated. All I could see was a cultured, well-bred young man, the very last word in refinement, and I couldn't care less about his rank.

MAYOR. Huh, women! That's typical. It's all one big joke to you, all fuss and feathers! There's no telling what you'll come out with. You'll give the whole show away, and you'll get off with a whipping, while your poor husband cops it. Good God, you've been as free with him as if he were Dobchinsky or somebody.

ANNA. Oh, come, you needn't concern yourself on that score. We women know a thing or two. (*Looks at her daughter.*)

MAYOR (*aside*). It's a waste of time talking to you! This is a strange business altogether. I'm still half-dead from fright. (*Opens the door and calls out.*) Mishka, go and fetch constables Svistunov and Derzhimorda – they're outside the gates somewhere, not far. (*After a brief silence.*) Honestly, the whole world's gone to the dogs. You'd think people would at least *look* the part, but when you get some pathetic, skinny creature – how are you supposed to tell? I mean, you can spot a military man right away, but you put him in a frock coat, and he looks like a fly with its wings clipped. He certainly put up a brave show at the hotel, all those cock-and-bull stories and logic-chopping – I thought I'd never get

to the bottom of him. But he caved in at last, and now he's
let slip more than he should have. Yes, a *young* man,
obviously.

OSIP *enters. They all rush up to him, beckoning.*

ANNA. Come over here, my dear fellow!

MAYOR. Sshhh! Well? Well? Is he asleep?

OSIP. Not yet – he's having a bit of a stretch.

ANNA. Now tell me, what's your name?

OSIP. It's Osip, ma'am.

MAYOR (*To his wife and daughter*). Right, you two, that's enough!
(*To* OSIP.) Now then, friend, are they feeding you properly?

OSIP. They are indeed, sir, thank you very much.

ANNA. And tell me this – I suppose your master has ever so
many counts and princes calling on him?

OSIP (*aside*). What'll I say? If they're feeding me well now, they
might feed me even better. (*Aloud.*) Oh yes, ma'am, counts
and everything.

MARYA. Oh, dear Osip, your master's so handsome!

ANNA. And tell me, Osip, please, how does he . . .

MAYOR. That's enough, do you hear! You're putting me off
with your silly chatter. Now then, friend . . .

ANNA. And what rank is your master?

OSIP. Well, the usual rank, I suppose.

MAYOR. God almighty, will you stop badgering him with your
stupid questions! I can't get a word in edgewise. Now, listen,
friend – what's your master like? Is he very strict? Does he
bawl people out?

OSIP. Oh yes, he's a real stickler. Got to have everything just
so.

MAYOR. You know, I like the look of you. You strike me as a decent chap. Anyway . . .

ANNA. Osip, Osip, listen – what does your master wear when he's at home, does he have a uniform, or . . .

MAYOR. Will you give over! Honestly, talk about chatterboxes! This is a serious matter – a man's life's at stake here . . . (*To* OSIP.) Anyway, friend, as I was saying, I've taken a real liking to you. You know, the odd glass of tea never comes amiss, when you're on the road this weather, so here's a couple of silver ones for your trouble.

OSIP (*accepting the coins*). Thank you very much, sir, God bless you. You've done a poor man a kindness.

MAYOR. Not at all, it's my pleasure. Anyway, friend, as I was . . .

ANNA. Osip, listen to me – what colour eyes does your master like best?

MARYA. Oh, Osip darling, hasn't your master the sweetest little nose!

MAYOR. For God's sake, will you let me speak! (*To* OSIP.) Listen, friend, tell me, please – what sort of things does your master notice? What does he particularly like, when he's on his travels?

OSIP. Well, that depends. He takes things as he finds them, but he likes to be looked after – the hospitality's got to be top class.

MAYOR. Top class?

OSIP. The hospitality, yes. I mean, you look at me, I'm just a serf, but he makes sure I'm treated right, I swear to God he does. We can pay a call on some place, and he'll say: 'Well, Osip, did they look after you all right?' And I'll say: 'No, your Honour, it was rotten.' 'Ooh, that's bad, Osip', he'll say, 'I don't like that. Just you remind me when we get back to Petersburg.' But I think to myself, well, what's the odds. (*Waves his hand dismissively.*) I'm a simple man, sir.

MAYOR. That's good, that's good, that makes sense. Osip, I've just given you some money for tea, so here you are, here's a bit extra for a bun.

OSIP. I don't know why you're so good to me, your Honour. (*Puts the money away.*) But I'll certainly drink to your health.

ANNA. If you come to my room, Osip, I'll give you something too.

MARYA. Oh Osip, dearest, kiss your master for me!

A faint cough is heard from KHLESTAKOV *in the other room.*

MAYOR. Ssshh! (*Goes on tiptoe, everyone speaks in a whisper.*) For heaven's sake don't make a noise! Now clear off, both of you.

ANNA. Come on, Masha dear, let's go. There's something I noticed about our guest, but I can't tell you till we're on our own, just the two of us. (*They exit.*)

MAYOR. Honestly, they'd talk the hind legs off a donkey! They'd give you earache, I swear to God. (*Turns to* OSIP.) Now then, friend . . .

Enter Constables DERZHIMORDA *and* SVISTUNOV.

Ssshh! You clumsy oafs! Clumping around in those damn boots! My God, you come crashing in here, it's like somebody chucking half-ton weights off a cart! Where the hell have you been?

DERZHIMORDA. Sir, in accordance with instructions, I was . . .

MAYOR (*Claps his hand over his mouth*). Ssshh! You sound like a damn crow! Caw! Caw! (*Mimics him.*) 'In accordance with instructions!' And that voice, coming up out of your boots! (*To* OSIP.) Now, off you go, friend, you make sure your master has everything he needs in there. If there's anything we haven't got, just ask. (OSIP *exits.*) As for you two – stay out on the porch and don't budge! Don't let anybody in, especially not shopkeepers! You let one of those creatures in,

and by God . . . The minute you see anybody coming up
with a petition, or even if they haven't got one – supposing
they just *look* as if they might have a petition – then grab him
by the scruff of the neck and kick him out! Like this! Good
and proper! (*Demonstrates with his foot.*) D'you hear? Now,
ssshh! Ssshh! (*Exits on tiptoe after the* CONSTABLES.)

Curtain.

Act Four

The same room in the MAYOR's *house. Cautiously, almost on tiptoe, enter the* JUDGE, *the* CHARITIES WARDEN, *the* POSTMASTER, *the* SCHOOLS SUPERINTENDENT, DOBCHINSKY *and* BOBCHINSKY, *all in full dress uniform. The entire scene is played in hushed voices.*

JUDGE (*organizes everybody into a semi-circle*). Gentlemen, for goodness' sake, hurry up and form a circle, let's have a bit more order! God save us, this is a man who drives to the Palace and tears strips off the Privy Council! Get into battle order, come on, line up! No, Bobchinsky, you run round to this side, and you stay where you are, Dobchinsky.

BOBCHINSKY *and* DOBCHINSKY *both run round on tiptoe.*

WARDEN. It's up to you, Judge, but we really ought to arrange something.

JUDGE. What do you mean exactly?

WARDEN. Well, you know . . .

JUDGE. What, a bribe?

WARDEN. Yes, a backhander, you know . . .

JUDGE. No, too risky, dammit. He'll howl the place down, a Government man. Not unless we make a donation, say, from the local gentry, towards some monument or other.

POSTMASTER. What if we say: 'Look, here's some money just arrived through the post, we've no idea who it belongs to'?

WARDEN. Yes, well, you'd better watch he doesn't post *you*, to some far-off land! Listen, in a well-ordered society people don't do these things . And what are we all lined up here for, like a cavalry charge? We ought to present ourselves to him one by one, so it's private, and, er . . . to keep things right – so other people can't hear. That's what happens in a well-ordered society. Right then, Judge – you can go first.

JUDGE. No no – it's better if you go. After all, our distinguished visitor did break bread in your hospital.

WARDEN. Actually, the Superintendent should go first, as the torch-bearer to our youth.

SUPERINTENDENT. No, I can't, sirs – I can't do it. Perhaps it's my upbringing, but honestly, the minute someone even one rank higher than me starts speaking, my mind goes blank, and I get completely tongue-tied. No, sirs, please, count me out!

WARDEN. Well, Judge, I suppose that leaves you. Go on, you'd even be a match for Cicero.

JUDGE. Oh, rubbish! Cicero, really! Just because a man gets carried away now and again, talking about his dogs, or a fine bloodhound . . .

ALL (*urging him*). No, no, Judge – not just dogs, you could've talked up the Tower of Babel! Judge, please, don't let us down, you're like a father to us! Please, don't abandon us!

JUDGE. Gentlemen, leave me be!

Just then, footsteps and coughing are heard from KHLESTAKOV's *room. They all make a mad rush to escape from the room, bunching together, and some of them become wedged in the door. Stifled cries of pain.*

BOBCHINSKY. Ouch! Dobchinsky, you're standing on my foot!

WARDEN. Let me through, sirs, have a heart! You're squeezing me to death!

More cries of 'Ouch!, etc., until finally all manage to squeeze out, leaving the room empty. KHLESTAKOV *then emerges, bleary-eyed.*

KHLESTAKOV. Well, I must've had a decent snooze. I
wonder where they got those mattresses and eiderdowns? I'm
dripping with sweat. I think they must've slipped me
something at lunch yesterday – my head's still thumping.
Yes, from what I've seen, I could pass the time very
pleasantly here. I do enjoy hospitality, and all the more so
when it's out of the goodness of people's hearts, and not
some ulterior motive. The Mayor's daughter's not bad-
looking, and his wife'd do a turn, too . . . I don't know, I
quite fancy this way of life.

The JUDGE *enters, and stops by the door.*

JUDGE (*aside*). Oh Lord, oh Lord! Help me out here, please!
My knees are giving way . . . (*Aloud, drawing himself up to his
full height, his hand on his sword-hilt.*) Sir, permit me to introduce
myself – Collegiate Assessor, and presiding Judge of the
District Court – Lyapkin-Tyapkin.

KHLESTAKOV. Sit down, please. So – you're the law in these
parts?

JUDGE. Yes, sir – appointed in 1816 for a three-year term, at
the instance of the local nobility, and continued in that post
until the present.

KHLESTAKOV. I see. And is it a profitable business, being a
judge?

JUDGE. Well, sir, after three full terms of office I was
recommended for the Order of St Vladimir, Fourth Class,
with my superiors' approval. (*Aside.*) Oh Lord, this money's
burning a hole in my fist!

KHLESTAKOV. Oh, I do like the Vladimir. It leaves the St
Anne Third Class simply nowhere.

JUDGE (*slowly extending his clenched fist. Aside*). God Almighty – I
feel as if I'm sitting on hot coals!

KHLESTAKOV. What's that you have in your hand?

JUDGE (*panics, and drops the banknotes on the floor*). Nothing, sir!

KHLESTAKOV. What d'you mean nothing? Didn't I see money falling?

JUDGE (*trembling all over*). No no, it was absolutely nothing, sir! (*Aside.*) Oh Lord, I'm in the dock now! And the cart's arrived to whisk me off to jail!

KHLESTAKOV (*Picking it up*). Yes, it is money.

JUDGE (*aside*). The game's up! I'm done for!

KHLESTAKOV. Look, I'll tell you what – why don't you give me a loan of this?

JUDGE (*eagerly*). Oh yes, sir, yes! With the greatest of pleasure! (*Aside.*) Now, go to it! Holy Mother of God, see me through this!

KHLESTAKOV. I ran out of cash on the road, you see, what with one thing and another . . . Anyway, I'll send it back to you from my estate.

JUDGE. Oh, please, don't even mention it – I'm only too honoured. Naturally, I endeavour to serve my superiors to the utmost of my abilities, meagre though they be . . . (*Rises from his chair and comes to attention.*) Sir, I shall not presume to trouble you further with my presence. Does Your Honour have any instructions for me?

KHLESTAKOV. What sort of instructions?

JUDGE. Well, I thought you might perhaps have some instructions for the District Court?

KHLESTAKOV. What on earth for? I've no business in that place now, surely?

JUDGE (*bows and makes to exit. Aside*). Yes, we've won the day!

KHLESTAKOV (*After he has gone*). Decent chap, the Judge.

Enter the POSTMASTER, *stiffly, his hand on his sword-hilt.*

POSTMASTER. Sir, permit me to introduce myself – Postmaster and Court Councillor Shpyokin.

KHLESTAKOV. Ah, I'm delighted to meet you. I do enjoy good company. Please, sit down. So, you've always lived here?

POSTMASTER. That's correct, Your Honour.

KHLESTAKOV. Yes, I rather like this little town. Not many people, of course, but so what? It's not the capital. It's not exactly St Petersburg, is it?

POSTMASTER. That's perfectly true, sir.

KHLESTAKOV. Yes, the capital's your only place for *le bon ton* – none of your provincial clods there, eh? What's your opinion?

POSTMASTER. That's absolutely right, sir. (*Aside.*) Well, one thing – he isn't too proud to ask questions.

KHLESTAKOV. Even so, you can live quite contentedly in a small town, wouldn't you say?

POSTMASTER. Yes, indeed, sir.

KHLESTAKOV. You know what I think? I think all you need is a bit of respect, a bit of sincere affection, *n'est-ce pas?*

POSTMASTER. I couldn't agree more, sir.

KHLESTAKOV. You know, I'm really pleased we're of the same mind. Of course, people will say I'm a queer fish, but that's just how I am. (*Peers closely at him, then aside.*) I think I'll tap this Postmaster for a loan! (*Aloud.*) You know, it's the damndest thing: I absolutely ran out of cash on the road. I don't suppose you could see your way to lending me three hundred roubles?

POSTMASTER. Yes, why not? With the greatest of pleasure, sir. Here, take it, please. I'm delighted to be of service.

KHLESTAKOV. Thank you very much. I must confess, I positively loathe having to do without things when I'm travelling, and why on earth should I? D'you agree?

POSTMASTER. Oh, completely, sir. (*Stands up, and comes to attention, his hand on his sword-hilt.*) Sir, I shall not presume to trouble you further with my presence. Does Your Honour wish to make any observations pertaining to the postal administration?

KHLESTAKOV. No, none at all.

The POSTMASTER *bows and exits.*

The Postmaster seems a decent chap too. Obliging, at any rate. My sort of people.

Enter the SUPERINTENDENT, *virtually shoved through the door. A voice is almost audible behind him: 'What are you scared of?' The* SUPERINTENDENT *comes to attention, hand on sword-hilt, in a state of some trepidation.*

SUPERINTENDENT. Sir, permit me to introduce myself – Superintendent of Schools and Titular Councillor Khlopov.

KHLESTAKOV. Pleased to meet you! Sit down, sit down. Would you care for a cigar? (*Offers him a cigar.*)

SUPERINTENDENT (*aside, indecisive*). Oh Lord, what now! I never expected this. Should I take it or shouldn't I?

KHLESTAKOV. Go on, take it, man. It's not a bad smoke. Not up to Petersburg standard, of course. No, old chap, I used to pay twenty-five roubles a hundred, really fine cigars – my God, you'd feel like kissing your hands after you'd smoked one. Here, light up. (*Hands him a candle.*)

The SUPERINTENDENT *tries to light the cigar, trembling all over.*

No, that's the wrong end, man!

The SUPERINTENDENT *drops the cigar out of sheer fright, spits, and flaps his arms.*

SUPERINTENDENT (*aside*). Damn these nerves of mine! They'll ruin everything!

KHLESTAKOV. Well, I can see you're not a cigar hand. I must admit they're one of my weaknesses. That and the fair sex, of course – I can't say I'm indifferent to them. What about you? Which do you prefer – blondes or brunettes?

The SUPERINTENDENT *is completely at a loss.*

Come on, man, out with it – blondes or brunettes?

SUPERINTENDENT. I wouldn't presume to know, sir.

KHLESTAKOV. Come on, you're not going to weasel out of it. I absolutely insist on knowing your preference.

SUPERINTENDENT. Well, sir, if I might venture an opinion . . . (*Aside.*) Oh Lord, I don't know *what* to say!

KHLESTAKOV. Aha! You won't tell, eh? Why, I'll wager some little brunette's got her claws into you. She has, hasn't she – come on, admit it!

The SUPERINTENDENT *is silent.*

Ho-ho! You're blushing! You see? You see? Why won't you tell me?

SUPERINTENDENT. Your Hon . . . Your Gra . . . Your High . . . Oh, I'm too afraid! (*Aside.*) This damn tongue's let me down again!

KHLESTAKOV. Afraid? Yes, I suppose there is something in my eyes that makes people go a bit weak at the knees. Certainly I know the ladies can't resist them, am I right?

SUPERINTENDENT. Oh, absolutely correct, sir.

KHLESTAKOV. Well, anyway, it's the damnedest thing, but would you believe, I got competely wiped out on the road. You couldn't lend me three hundred roubles, I suppose?

SUPERINTENDENT (*groping in his pockets, aside*). Oh Lord, what if I haven't got it! Yes, yes, it's here! (*Pulls out some banknotes and hands them over, trembling.*)

KHLESTAKOV. Thank you very much.

SUPERINTENDENT (*comes to attention, hand on sword-hilt*). Sir, I shall not presume to trouble you further with my presence.

KHLESTAKOV. Goodbye!

SUPERINTENDENT (*practically flies out of the room. Aside*). Thank God for that! With any luck he won't even look at the school.

Enter the CHARITIES WARDEN, *who comes to attention, hand on sword-hilt.*

WARDEN. Sir, permit me to introduce myself: Warden of Charitable Institutions, Court Councillor Zemlyanika.

KHLESTAKOV. Good morning. Do sit down, please.

WARDEN. I had the honour to receive you in person, sir, and accompany you on your inspection of those institutions entrusted to my care.

KHLESTAKOV. Oh yes, I remember now. You did us a very decent lunch.

WARDEN. I am only too pleased to be of service to my country.

KHLESTAKOV. Yes, I must confess that's one of my weaknesses − I do like good food. Actually, I had the impression you were a little bit shorter yesterday − was I right?

WARDEN. Quite possibly, sir. (*After a pause.*) I can truthfully say I never spare myself in the execution of my duties. (*Draws his chair a little closer and speaks in a half-whisper.*) Actually, the Postmaster here does absolutely nothing. The whole business is in an advanced state of neglect, parcels get held up . . . you might well investigate that. The Judge too, who was in here just before me, spends all his time hare-coursing, and keeps his hounds in the court-house, and as for his conduct − I feel obliged to say this, of course, only for the good of my country, although he's my own kith and kin, and a friend − well, his conduct is utterly reprehensible. There's a certain landowner here, Dobchinsky – I believe you've met him, sir – well, no sooner does Dobchinsky step out of the house, than the Judge is sitting there with his wife. And I'm ready to swear to that, sir – you just take a look at the children: not one of them looks like Dobchinsky, they're all the spitting image of the Judge, even the little girl!

KHLESTAKOV. You don't say! I'd never have believed it.

WARDEN. And then there's our Superintendent of Schools . . . I don't know how the authorities could have entrusted him with such a position. He's worse than a French revolutionary, he fills our young people's heads with such pernicious ideas that I hardly dare utter them aloud. Perhaps you'd like me to put all this down on paper?

KHLESTAKOV. Yes, on paper, by all means. That'll be splendid. I really enjoy having something amusing to read when I'm bored. By the way, what's your name? I keep forgetting.

WARDEN. It's Zemlyanika, sir.

KHLESTAKOV. Ah yes, Zemlyanika. And tell me, do you have any children?

COMMISSONER. Indeed I have, sir – five. Two of them already grown up.

KHLESTAKOV. Grown up, fancy that! So what are they . . . er, what are their . . . ?

WARDEN. I take it Your Honour is enquiring as to their names?

KHLESTAKOV. Yes, what are they called?

WARDEN. Nikolai, Ivan, Yelizaveta, Marya, and Perepetuya.

KHLESTAKOV. That's nice.

WARDEN. Sir, I shall not presume to trouble you further with my presence, taking up time which I'm sure you have allotted to your sacred duties . . . (*Bows and makes to leave.*)

KHLESTAKOV (*accompanying him to the door*). Think nothing of it. It's all very amusing, what you've been saying. Do please come again. I've enjoyed this hugely. (*Turns back and opens the door, calls after him.*) Wait, hold on! Who did you say you were? I keep forgetting your name.

WARDEN. It's Zemlyanika, sir. Artemy Filipovich.

KHLESTAKOV. Well, look, Artemy old chap, it's the damndest thing, but I got cleaned out competely on the road. You haven't any money you could lend me – say, four hundred roubles?

WARDEN. I have, sir.

KHLESTAKOV. Really? That's very handy. Thank you so much.

The WARDEN *hands over the money and exits. Enter* BOBCHINSKY *and* DOBCHINSKY.

BOBCHINSKY. Sir, permit me to introduce myself: Pyotr Ivanovich Bobchinsky, resident of this town.

DOBCHINSKY. And Pyotr Ivanovich Dobchinsky, landowner.

KHLESTAKOV (*To* BOBCHINSKY). Ah yes, I've seen you before. You fell over, I think. So, how's the nose?

BOBCHINSKY. Oh, don't concern yourself, sir. It's healed up now, thank goodness, dry as a bone.

KHLESTAKOV. Good, I'm glad to hear it. Yes, delighted . . . (*Abruptly.*) Got any money on you?

BOBCHINSKY. Money? What for?

KHLESTAKOV (*rapidly*). For a loan of a thousand roubles.

BOBCHINSKY. Good heavens, I don't have that kind of money. What about you, Dobchinsky?

DOBCHINSKY. No, sir, nor do I, to be honest. All my money's lodged with the Board of Guardians, doing good works, you see.

KHLESTAKOV. Well, if you can't run to a thousand, make it a hundred.

BOBCHINSKY (*rummaging in his pockets*). Dobchinsky, you haven't got a hundred roubles, have you? All I've got is forty in notes.

DOBCHINSKY (*looks in his wallet*). Twenty-five, and that's the lot.

BOBCHINSKY. Have another look, Dobchinsky, for heaven's sake! You've got a hole in your right-hand pocket, I know you have. It's probably slipped through.

DOBCHINSKY. No, there's nothing there, honestly.

KHLESTAKOV. Well, no matter. I'll get by. You can let me have the sixty-five roubles, that'll be fine. (*Takes the money.*)

DOBCHINSKY. Sir, if I might make so bold as to ask your assistance on a rather delicate matter . . .

KHLESTAKOV. Yes, what is it?

DOBCHINSKY. Really, it's an extremely delicate business: you see, my eldest boy, Your Honour, was born out of wedlock.

KHLESTAKOV. Indeed?

DOBCHINSKY. Well, in a manner of speaking, that is – he was born just the same as if it were in wedlock, and I put everything to rights afterwards, Your Honour, within the bonds of matrimony, so to speak. Anyway, if you could see your way clear, Your Honour – what I'd like now is for him to be my son and heir – legitimate, I mean – and take my name – Dobchinsky.

KHLESTAKOV. Fine, let him take it. No problem.

DOBCHINSKY. I wouldn't have troubled Your Honour, but it's a real shame, on acccount of his abilities. He's a remark-able lad, shows great promise: he can recite all sorts of poems by heart, and he's only got to pick up a penknife, and he'll carve you a tiny little droshky quick as a flash. Bobchinsky'll tell you.

BOBCHINSKY. Yes, he's a talented lad.

KHLESTAKOV. Good, good! I'll see what I can do, I'll have a word with . . . I'm sure I can . . . oh, I'll sort something out, yes, of course. (*Turns to* BOBCHINSKY.) And what about you? Have you nothing for me?

BOBCHINSKY. Well, sir, when you go back to Petersburg, I'd be most deeply grateful if you'd just say to all those bigwigs there, all those senators and admirals: 'Look, Your Highness, or Your Excellency or whatever, there's this town, and there's a chap called Bobchinsky living there . . . ' Just say: 'There's a chap called Bobchinsky.'

KHLESTAKOV. Fine, I'll do that.

BOBCHINSKY. And if you should happen to run into the Emperor, then tell him too. Say: 'You know, Your Imperial Majesty, there's a certain town, and there's a chap called Bobchinsky.'

KHLESTAKOV. Fine, I'll do that.

DOBCHINSKY. Sir, I do apologise for burdening you with my presence.

BOBCHINSKY. Sir, I do apologise for burdening you with my presence.

KHLESTAKOV. Not at all. It's been my pleasure. (*Shows them out, then to himself.*) Well, there's a lot of civil servants in this place. I think they must've mistaken me for some high Government official. True enough, I did put on the dog a bit yesterday. What imbeciles! I must drop a note to Tryapichkin in Petersburg about this. He writes all those articles – he'll make mincemeat out of this lot. Hey, Osip, fetch me some paper and ink! (OSIP *pops his head round the door, says: 'Right, sir!'*.) By God, once Tryapichkin gets his teeth into you – watch out! He wouldn't even spare his own father, if there was a joke in it, and he's not averse to cash, either. Actually, these people are quite decent. After all, they have been lending me money, that's a point in their favour, surely. I'd better

check, see how much I've got. Now, that's three hundred
from the Judge, three hundred from the Postmaster – that
makes six hundred . . . seven hundred . . . eight hundred . . .
ugh, what a greasy note! . . . eight hundred . . . nine hundred . . . ho-ho! That's over a thousand! By God, just let that
infantry captain turn up now. We'll see who gets skinned this
time!

Enter OSIP *with ink and paper.*

Now, you oaf, you see? You see how well I'm looked after?
(*Begins writing.*)

OSIP. I do, thanks be to God. But I'll tell you something,
master.

KHLESTAKOV. Oh, and what's that?

OSIP. You want to clear off out of here. While the going's
good, believe me.

KHLESTAKOV. Oh, rubbish! What for?

OSIP. Because. Just cut and run, sir. We've had a right good
couple of days here, and that'll do us. You don't want any
more dealings with these people – to hell with 'em! It'd be
just our luck if somebody was to turn up. Honest to God,
master! And they've got some dandy horses, we'd be out of
here in no time.

KHLESTAKOV (*writing*). No, I think I'll hang around a bit
longer. Maybe tomorrow.

OSIP. What d'you mean tomorrow? Master, let's go now, for
God's sake! All right, so they're treating you like royalty, but
the sooner we make tracks the better. It's obvious they've
mistaken you for somebody else. And your father'll be
spitting mad if we don't get a move on. We could roll out of
here in style – they'd give us top-class horses.

KHLESTAKOV. Oh, all right then. Just take this letter first,
and you might as well order the post-horses while you're at
it. And make sure they're the best! Tell the coachmen I'll

give them a rouble apiece, to drive me like one of His Majesty's couriers, and sing songs on the way! (*Continues writing.*) Tryapichkin'll die laughing, I can just imagine . . .

OSIP. Sir, I'll send one of the men here with this, I'll get busy with the packing, so we don't waste any time.

KHLESTAKOV (*writing*). Fine, fine – just bring me a candle.

OSIP (*exits and speaks off-stage*). Hey, you – listen! You've to take a letter to the post office, and tell the Postmaster he's not to charge for it. Yes, and tell him to send round his best troika – same as he keeps for the couriers – and the gentleman's not paying the hire on that neither. It's official business, tell him. Now come on, look lively, afore his lordship loses his temper. Wait, wait – the letter's not finished yet.

KHLESTAKOV (*continuing to write*). I wonder where he's staying these days – Post Office Street or Gorokhovaya? He's another one for changing his lodgings, and not paying his rent. Well, I'll address it to Post Office Street on the off-chance. (*Folds the letter and addresses it.*)

OSIP *brings the candle, and* KHLESTAKOV *seals up the letter. Just then, Constable* DERZHIMORDA *is heard outside: 'Hey, you with the beard – where d'you think you're going? Nobody's allowed in here, that's orders.'* KHLESTAKOV *hands* OSIP *the letter.*

Right, take it away.

SHOPKEEPERS (*off-stage*). Let us through, sir. You can't keep us out. We're here on business.

DERZHIMORDA (*off-stage*). Clear off! Come on, break it up! He's not seeing anybody, he's asleep.

The hubbub increases.

KHLESTAKOV. What's going on out there, Osip? See what that noise is.

OSIP (*looks out of the window*). It's shopkeepers, sir, and the like – they're trying to come in but the constable won't let 'em. They're waving bits of paper: I think they want to see you.

KHLESTAKOV (*goes over to the window*). Yes, what is it you want, dear friends?

SHOPKEEPERS (*off-stage*). Your Honour, we've come to beg a favour. Tell them to let us in, sir – receive our petitions.

KHLESTAKOV. Let these men in, d'you hear! Let them in. Osip, tell them to come in.

OSIP *exits*. KHLESTAKOV *accepts the petitions through the window, opens one and begins reading it.*

'From the merchant Abdulin, to His Most Serene Magnificence, the Lord High Financier . . .' What the devil's this? There's no such personage.

The SHOPKEEPERS *enter, carrying a basket of wine and sugar-loaves.*

KHLESTAKOV. Now, what can I do for you, my dear sirs?

SHOPKEEPERS. Your Honour, we most humbly crave your indulgence!

KHLESTAKOV. What is it you want?

SHOPKEEPERS. Save us from ruin, sir! We're being shamefully abused, for no reason.

KHLESTAKOV. By whom?

A SHOPKEEPER. It's all because of the Mayor here, sir. There's never been a mayor like him, Your Honour. The things he gets away with, you wouldn't believe. He billets soldiers in our homes, sir – honestly, you might as well put your head in a noose. He just doesn't know when to stop. He'll grab you by the beard and shout: 'Come on, you heathen!' Honest to God, sir! I mean, if we'd been disrespectful, fair enough, but we've always done right by him: a bit of dress material for his wife and daughter – we don't mind that at all. But oh no, that's not enough for him. No, he just walks into the shop and takes whatever he fancies. He'll see a bolt of cloth, he'll say: 'You've some nice

stuff there, my good man – send that round to me, will you?'
So you've got to take it round, and there's all of fifty yards in
that piece.

KHLESTAKOV. Really? Why, the man's a scoundrel!

SHOPKEEPERS. Honest to God, sir! Nobody can remember a
mayor like him. You have to hide everything in the shop, the
minute you see him coming. And he's not fussy, either, he'll
take any old rubbish: prunes, say, that've been lying in the
barrel for seven years, that even my message-boy wouldn't
touch, and he'll eat them by the fistful! His name-day falls on
St Anton's, and of course, you shower him with presents,
you'd think he lacked for nothing, but no, you've got to do
the same again – he says his name-day's St Hilarios as well!
And what can you do, except give him more presents?

KHLESTAKOV. Highway robbery!

SHOPKEEPERS. Too true! And if you dare say a word against
him, he'll billet a whole regiment on you. Either that or he'll
close you down. 'I can't order corporal punishment,' he'll tell
you, 'Or have you tortured, because that's against the law,
but by God,' he'll say, 'You'll be on bread and water, if it's
up to me!'

KHLESTAKOV. Conniving wretch, he should go straight to
Siberia!

SHOPKEEPERS. Or anywhere Your Honour cares to send
him, that's fine by us, as long as it's far away. Now, good sir,
please don't turn down our hospitality – see, we've brought
you a little hamper of wine, and some sugar-loaves.

KHLESTAKOV. Heavens no, don't even think of it: I don't
accept any sort of bribes. On the other hand, if you were to
offer me a loan, say, of three hundred roubles – well, that's a
different matter. Loans I can accept.

SHOPKEEPERS. Oh, please do, Your Honour! (*Fishing out
money.*) And why only three hundred? Take five hundred,
better still – just help us, please!

KHLESTAKOV. Well, I won't say no – but it's a loan, mind.

SHOPKEEPERS (*presenting him with the money on a silver tray*). Here you are, Your Honour, and please, keep the tray.

KHLESTAKOV. Mm, I suppose I can..

SHOPKEEPERS (*bowing*). And take the sugar-loaves along with it.

KHLESTAKOV. No no, I don't accept bribes.

OSIP. Oh, go on, take it, Your Magnificence – why not? Take it! It'll come in handy on the road. Look, give me the sugar, and the bag. I'll take the lot, it won't go to waste. What's that, string? Give me that as well – you can always find a use for a bit of string, like say, if the waggon comes apart or something, you can tie it up.

SHOPKEEPERS. So you'll look kindly on our petition, Your Excellency? Truly, if you can't help us, we don't know what we'll do – stick our heads in a noose, most like.

KHLESTAKOV. Oh, for sure, absolutely. I'll do my level best.

The SHOPKEEPERS *exit. A woman's voice is heard off-stage: 'Don't you dare keep me out! I'll complain to His Honour about you too! Ow! Don't push, you're hurting me!'*

Who's that? (*Crosses to the window*). What's the matter, woman?

TWO WOMEN (*off-stage*). Have mercy on us, Your Honour, please! Tell 'em to let us in, sir – give us a hearing!

KHLESTAKOV (*through the window*). Let them in.

Enter the LOCKSMITH'S WIFE *and the* SERGEANT'S WIDOW.

LOCKSMITH'S WIFE (*bowing deeply*). Oh, sir, I beg you . . .

SERGEANT'S WIDOW. Have mercy on us!

KHLESTAKOV. Who are you good women?

SERGEANT'S WIDOW. Sir, I'm Sergeant Ivanov's widow.

LOCKSMITH'S WIFE. And I'm a local woman, Your Honour – Fevronya Poshlyopkin, the locksmith's wife.

KHLESTAKOV. Hold on, one at a time, please. What is it you want?

LOCKSMITH'S WIFE. Have mercy on me, sir: I want to complain about the Mayor, God rot him! May he rot in hell, sir, him and his brats and his whole tribe, aunts and uncles and all – I hope they get no good out of nothing, not ever!

KHLESTAKOV. Heavens, why not?

LOCKSMITH'S WIFE. 'Cause he had my husband called up into the army, sir, the thieving swine, and it weren't his turn, neither. He's a married man, Your Honour, it ain't legal.

KHLESTAKOV. How'd he manage that, for God's sake?

LOCKSMITH'S WIFE. Oh, he managed, sir, the scheming rat – may God strike him down, in this world and the next, yes! I hope he meets a bad end, sir, him and his aunt, if he's got one, yes, and his father, if he's still alive – I hope he snuffs it too, the miserable old crow, I hope he chokes on his porridge! He was supposed to send the tailor's boy, he's a drunken pig anyway, but his folks've got money, they bought him off, so then he picks on old Panteleeva's son, her that keeps the shop, and Panteleeva sends the Mayor's wife three bolts of cloth, so he's onto me next. 'What d'you need a husband for anyway?' he says, 'He's no use to you.' Well, whether he's any use or not, I says, that's my business, you conniving old villain! 'He's a thief,' he says, 'And if he hasn't stolen anything yet, he soon enough will, and he'll be conscripted next year anyway, so what's the odds?' 'And what am I supposed to do with no husband, I says, you rotten crook? I'm a poor weak woman, you miserable wretch! By God, I hope none of your family ever sees the light of day again! And if you've got a mother-in-law, I hope she . . .'

KHLESTAKOV. Yes, yes, I get the gist. Well, then – and what about you? (*Showing the* LOCKSMITH'S WIFE *out.*)

LOCKSMITH'S WIFE. Don't forget, please, Your Honour! Have mercy on us!

SERGEANT'S WIDOW. Sir, I've come about the Mayor too . . .

KHLESTAKOV. Well, get on with it then – and keep it short.

SERGEANT'S WIDOW. He had me flogged, Your Honour!

KHLESTAKOV. What?

SERGEANT'S WIDOW. It was all a mistake, sir. Some of us women was having a bit of a set-to at the market, and the police didn't turn up in time, so they just grabbed me for it. Beat the living daylights out of me, they did – I couldn't sit down for a week.

KHLESTAKOV. So what can I do about it now?

SERGEANT'S WIDOW. There's not much you can do, sir, of course, but you can order him to pay me compensation for the mistake. I could do with a spot of luck right now, and the money would come in handy.

KHLESTAKOV. All right, fine. Now run along, and I'll see what I can do.

Various hands are thrusting petitions in through the window.

Who's this next? (*Crosses to the window.*) No, I don't want these! Take them away! (*Withdraws.*) Oh, to hell with this, I've had enough! Osip, don't let them in!

OSIP (*shouts through the window.*) Go away! Go on, clear off! Time's up, come back tomorrow!

The door opens to reveal a figure in a shoddy greatcoat, unshaven, with a swollen lip and a bandaged jaw. Several others can be seen in the background behind him.

Clear off, I said! Where d'you think you're going?

He gives the first man a shove in the stomach, and follows him out into the hall, slamming the door shut after him, and leaving KHLESTAKOV *alone on stage. Enter the Mayor's daughter,* MARYA.

MARYA. Oh!

KHLESTAKOV. Did I frighten you, dear lady?

MARYA. No, I'm not frightened.

KHLESTAKOV (*striking a pose*). I must say I'm rather pleased at being taken for the sort of man who . . . May I presume to ask where you were intending to go?

MARYA. Honestly, I wasn't going anywhere.

KHLESTAKOV. And why, indeed, weren't you going anywhere?

MARYA. I was just wondering if mama was here.

KHLESTAKOV. No no, I really would like to know *why* you weren't going anywhere.

MARYA. Sir, I've disturbed you. You have important business to attend to.

KHLESTAKOV (*striking another pose*). But aren't your lovely eyes more important than my business? There's no way you could disturb me, none whatsoever. On the contrary, you can afford me nothing but pleasure.

MARYA. Oh, you speak so beautifully – just like they do in Petersburg!

KHLESTAKOV. To so beautiful a creature as yourself, yes. May I make so bold as to offer you a chair? I should be so happy. Heavens, no – not a chair – for you, it should be a throne!

MARYA. Really, I don't know . . . I ought to be going, honestly. (*Sits.*)

KHLESTAKOV. What an exquisite scarf you're wearing!

MARYA. You're making fun of me – you like having a laugh at us provincials.

KHLESTAKOV. Oh, dear lady, how I long to be that scarf of yours, to embrace your lily-white neck.

MARYA. I can't imagine what you mean. It's just an old scarf – 'cause the weather's a bit up and down today.

KHLESTAKOV. My dear lady, what matter any kind of weather, beside your beautiful lips!

MARYA. Gracious, the things you say! I wouldn't mind asking you to write something in my album – some verses, for a keepsake. I bet you know lots of poems.

KHLESTAKOV. For you, sweet lady – anything, anything. What sort of verses would you like?

MARYA. Oh, any sort, I don't mind. Something nice and new.

KHLESTAKOV. Ah yes, verses, verses! I know heaps.

MARYA. Tell me what you're going to write – say them.

KHLESTAKOV. What's the point of reciting them? I know them well enough.

MARYA. I do so love poetry.

KHLESTAKOV. You see, I know so many – all sorts of poems. Oh, all right – what about this, then?

*'O, man, that in thy sorrows dost cry out
In vain upon the Lord thy God!'*

There's others besides, I just can't call them to mind. Anyway, that's neither here nor there. I'd much rather declare my love – the love I feel, gazing into your eyes . . . (*Moves his chair closer.*)

MARYA. Love! I don't understand love. I've never even known what it was. (*Moves her chair away.*)

KHLESTAKOV (*moving closer*). Why are you pulling your chair away? We'll be much cosier sitting close together.

MARYA (*moving away*). Why sit closer? Why not further away?

KHLESTAKOV (*moving closer*) .What d'you mean further away? Why not closer?

MARYA (*moving away*). What on earth are you up to?

KHLESTAKOV (*moving closer*). Believe me, you only imagine we're close together, so just imagine we're far apart instead. Oh, my dear lady, how happy I'd be if I could enfold you in my arms, and press you to my bosom!

MARYA (*looks out of the window*). Oh look, I'm sure that was a bird that just flew past. Was it a magpie, d'you think, or some other sort?

KHLESTAKOV (*kisses her shoulder, and looks out of the window*). It was a magpie.

MARYA (*springs up in indignation*). Oh, this is going too far! What a cheek!

KHLESTAKOV (*trying to restrain her*). Forgive me, dear lady! It was love that made me do it, nothing but love!

MARYA. Obviously you take me for some country wench, the sort who . . .

KHLESTAKOV (*still trying to restrain her*). It was love, I swear, simple affection. An innocent bit of fun, dearest lady, please don't be angry. I'll go down on my knees and beg your forgiveness! (*Kneels.*) Forgive me, please, please. Look, I'm on my knees to you.

Enter the Mayor's wife, ANNA.

ANNA (*seeing KHLESTAKOV on his knees*). Oh! What a scene!

KHLESTAKOV (*rising*). Damn!

ANNA (*to her daughter*). What's the meaning of this, young lady? What sort of behaviour do you call this?

MARYA. Mama, dearest, I . . .

ANNA. Get out of my sight! Get out, d'you hear! And don't dare show your face in here again! (*MARYA exits in tears.*) You'll forgive me, sir, but I must confess I'm quite taken aback . . .

KHLESTAKOV (*aside*). She's quite appetising herself – not bad at all. (*Drops to his knees again.*) Oh, dear lady, you see how I'm consumed with love!

ANNA. What are you doing on your knees? Stand up, stand up, for goodness' sake! I mean, the floor's not even clean.

KHLESTAKOV. No no, I must kneel, I absolutely must! I must know my fate – whether life, or death!

ANNA. I'm sorry, sir, but I'm not sure I fully understand you. If I'm not mistaken, you're making a declaration of love for my daughter.

KHLESTAKOV. No, no, it's you I'm in love with, ma'am – you! My life hangs by a thread. If you won't requite my undying love, then I am unworthy to walk this earth. I ask for your hand, with a fierce flame of love burning in my breast!

ANNA. Sir, if you'll permit me to observe, I am, in a manner of speaking – a married woman.

KHLESTAKOV. Who cares! True love knows no such distinctions. As the great Karamzin himself says: '*Tis but man's law condemns!* Madame, let us withdraw to some shady rill . . . your hand, I implore you, give me your hand!

MARYA suddenly rushes into the room.

MARYA. Mama, papa says you've got to . . . (*Seeing KHLESTAKOV on his knees, lets out a shriek.*) Oh! What a scene!

ANNA. What's the matter with you? What are you on about? Eh? Lord, what a silly creature! Running in here like a scalded cat – what are you standing there goggling at? What on earth's going on in that head of yours? Honestly, she's like a three-year-old infant. You'd never believe it – never in a month of Sundays would you believe she was eighteen years old! Heaven only knows when you're going to get some sense, and start behaving like a decent, well brought-up young woman! There are rules, you know, of good conduct and decorum – just when are you going to learn them?

MARYA (*in tears*). Mama, I had no idea . . .

ANNA. No, of course you hadn't – you've got nothing but air between your ears, that's why! You take your example from those Lyapkin-Tyapkin girls, the Judge's daughters. I don't know why you even look at them. Why copy them, for heaven's sake? It's not as if you've no better examples – your own mother, for a start, right here looking at you. That's the sort of example you should follow.

KHLESTAKOV (*seizing* MARYA's *hand*). Anna Andreevna, please don't stand in the way of our happiness. Give your blessing to our undying love!

ANNA (*bewildered*). What? So *she*'s the one . . . ?

KHLESTAKOV. Make your decision: life, or death!

ANNA. Well now, you see, you silly creature? You see what you've done? Because of you, all that stupid nonsense of yours, our guest has to go down on his knees, and you come rushing in like a mad thing. Honestly, I ought to refuse my consent. You just don't deserve such happiness.

MARYA. Oh, mama, I won't do it again. Truly I won't.

Enter the MAYOR, *out of breath.*

MAYOR. Oh, Your Excellency! Please don't ruin us! Don't destroy us, please!

KHLESTAKOV. What on earth's the matter?

MAYOR. It's those shopkeepers, sir – they've been complaining to Your Excellency. I swear to you on my honour, sir, you can't believe the half of what they say! They're the biggest cheats going, sir, them and their short weight. And the

sergeant's widow, the one I'm supposed to have flogged –
she's lying in her teeth, I swear to God. She flogged herself –
yes, she did!

KHLESTAKOV. Oh, the hell with your sergeant's widow –
what's she got to do with me?

MAYOR. Don't believe a word of it, Your Honour! They're
such damnable liars, sir – a babe in arms could see right
through them! They're famous for their lies, sir, the whole
town knows them. And when it comes to swindling, well, if I
may make so bold, Your Honour, you'll not find their equal
on land or sea!

ANNA. Anton, you surely can't be aware of the honour His
Excellency is bestowing upon us. He's asking for our
daughter's hand in marriage.

MAYOR. What! What! Good God, woman, have you gone
mad! Oh, Your Excellency, please don't be angry. She's not
right in the head, her mother was just the same.

KHLESTAKOV. No, it's true – I am asking for her hand. I'm
in love.

MAYOR. Your Excellency . . . I can't believe it.

ANNA. For heaven's sake, he's telling you!

KHLESTAKOV. I'm not joking, sir. I'm ready to run mad
with love.

MAYOR. No no, I daren't believe it, I'm not worthy of such an
honour.

KHLESTAKOV. Sir, if you don't consent to give me your
daughter's hand, God only knows what I'll do!

MAYOR. I can't believe it. You're pulling my leg, surely, Your
Excellency.

ANNA. Oh, you great stupid oaf! Why can't you get it into
your thick head?

MAYOR. I just can't believe it.

KHLESTAKOV. Your consent, for God's sake! I'm a desperate man, sir, I'm capable of anything. And when I shoot myself, it'll be your neck!

MAYOR. Oh, my God, please, no! I'm innocent, I swear, body and soul! Don't be angry, sir, please. Do whatever Your Honour sees fit, I beg you. To tell you the truth, my head's in an absolute . . . I haven't a clue what's going on. I've made a complete idiot of myself, the biggest idiot that ever was.

ANNA. Well, go on, give them your blessing!

KHLESTAKOV *steps forward with* MARYA.

MAYOR. God bless you both. I'm innocent, I tell you!

KHLESTAKOV *kisses* MARYA, *while the* MAYOR *looks on.*

What the devil! It is, it's true! (*Rubbing his eyes.*) They're actually kissing! Oh, my God, they're kissing! They're engaged! (*Shouts and jumps for joy.*) Oh, Anton, Anton! Yes, your worship! Yes, Mister Mayor! Now, there's a turn up!

OSIP *enters.*

OSIP. Sir, that's the horses ready.

KHLESTAKOV. Fine, I'll be down in a minute.

MAYOR. What's that, sir? You're not leaving?

KHLESTAKOV. Yes, I have to go.

MAYOR. But when, Your Honour? I mean, it was you yourself, sir, that was hinting about a wedding . . .

KHLESTAKOV. Oh yes, that . . . Look, I only need a minute . . . just a day or so to see my uncle – he's a wealthy old stick – and I'll be back without fail tomorrow.

MAYOR. Oh well, we wouldn't dream of detaining you, sir, and we'll look forward to Your Honour's safe return.

KHLESTAKOV. Yes, yes, of course – I'll be straight back. *Au revoir, mon amour!* No, no, I simply can't express what I feel! Goodbye, my darling! (*Kisses her hand.*)

MAYOR. Are you sure you don't need anything for the road, Your Honour? I believe you were a little short of cash?

KHLESTAKOV. Heavens no, where'd you get that idea? (*Thinks a moment.*) Well, possibly.

MAYOR. How much would you like?

KHLESTAKOV. Well, that two hundred you loaned me – or four hundred, I should say, I don't want to take advantage of your mistake – perhaps you could let me have the same again, make it a round eight hundred.

MAYOR. With pleasure! (*Takes the money out of his wallet.*) There you are, crisp new notes too, for the occasion.

KHLESTAKOV. Oh, yes. (*Accepts the notes and inspects them.*) These'll do nicely. Don't they say new notes bring you luck?

MAYOR. They do indeed, sir.

KHLESTAKOV. Well, goodbye, my dear friend. I'm much obliged to you for your hospitality. Yes, I must say in all sincerity, sir, I've never received such a warm welcome. (*To* ANNA.) Goodbye, dear lady! (*To* MARYA.) Goodbye, my darling!

All exit. For the remainder of the scene, their voices are heard off-stage.

KHLESTAKOV. Farewell, my angel, dearest Marya!

MAYOR. Good gracious, sir, you're surely not travelling in a post-chaise? They're so uncomfortable.

KHLESTAKOV. Oh, I'm used to that. I get a headache in a sprung carriage.

COACHMAN. Whoa, there!

MAYOR. Well, at the very least take something to spread on the seat, even just a rug. Shouldn't I order them to fetch Your Honour a rug?

KHLESTAKOV. No, it's not worth bothering about. Oh well, I suppose a rug wouldn't come amiss.

MAYOR. Hey, Avdotiya! Go into the store-room and bring out the best rug – the one with the blue background, the Persian. And look lively!

COACHMAN. Whoa, there!

MAYOR. So when may we expect Your Honour?

KHLESTAKOV. Oh, tomorrow or the next day.

OSIP. Is that the rug? Right, let's have it – put it down there. Now let's have a bit of hay round that side.

COACHMAN. Whoa, there!

OSIP. No, round this side! Here! A bit more. Right, that's fine. That'll do nicely. (*Pats the rug smooth.*) You can sit down now, Your Eminence.

KHLESTAKOV. Goodbye, my dear sir!

MAYOR. Goodbye, Your Excellency!

KHLESTAKOV. *Au revoir, chère maman!*

COACHMAN. Giddy up, my lovelies!

Harness bells ring as they drive off. Curtain.

Act Five

The same room. The MAYOR, *his wife* ANNA, *and daughter* MARYA.

MAYOR. Well, Anna my dear, what d'you think? Never
imagined anything like that, eh? Dammit, what a prize catch!
Come on, admit it – you'd never in your wildest dreams . . .
a simple town mayor's wife, and suddenly . . . Damn me, to
find yourself related to a young devil like that!

ANNA. Oh, nothing of the sort. I could see it coming ages ago.
Of course it's all marvellous to you, because you're just a
peasant, you've never mixed with decent people.

MAYOR. Now then, mother – I'm pretty decent myself.
Anyway, just think, Anna, we're birds of a different feather
now. What d'you think? By God, we're flying high all right!
Just wait, I'll give it hot to all those whingers with their
complaints and petitions. Hey! Who's out there? (*Enter the*
CONSTABLE.) Ah, it's you, Svistunov. Fetch all those
shopkeepers in here. By God, I'll sort them out, the rabble –
complain about me, would they? Well, you wait, you
damned Judases! Yes, you just wait, my darlings! I've given
you a hiding before now, but this time I'll pulverize you!
Make a note of their names, everybody that came here
whining about me, and those wretched scribblers, especially,
the ones that wrote out their complaints for them. Yes, and
make an announcement, let them all know what a great
honour God has bestowed on their Mayor – that he's
marrying his daughter not to some peasant, but a person the
like of which there's never been, a man who can do anything, absolutely anything! Announce it publicly, so they'll all
get the message. Shout it in the streets, ring the bells till they
crack, damn it! My God, if this isn't worth celebrating, then

what is! (*The* CONSTABLE *exits.*) Well now, Anna my dear, what d'you think? What'll we do now, eh? Where shall we live? Here or Petersburg, eh?

ANNA. Oh, St Petersburg, of course. We can't stay here!

MAYOR. All right, Petersburg it is. We could do nicely here too, though. Still, to hell with being mayor, that's what I say, right?

ANNA. Oh, a mayor – what's that!

MAYOR. I might land a plum job now, what d'you think, my dear? Because if he's hobnobbing with all the Ministers, and goes to Court and so on, well, he'll be able to wangle the odd promotion, I could even wind up a general. What d'you reckon, Anna – d'you think I'd make a general?

ANNA. Why shouldn't you! Of course you would.

MAYOR. Damn me, a general, that'd be marvellous! They hang a sash round your neck, you know, when you get promoted. Which d'you prefer, my dear, the red or the blue?

ANNA. Oh, the blue, of course.

MAYOR. Eh? You've set your heart on it? Well, the red's fine too. Anyway, d'you know why I fancy being a general? It's because whenever you go somewhere, couriers and adjutants and the like have to gallop on ahead, demanding horses! And they won't let anybody else have them at the staging-posts, they've all got to wait, all these councillors, captains, mayors, and you don't give a damn! You're having dinner with the Governor some place, and it's: 'Stand over there, Mister Mayor!' Hee, hee, hee! (*Goes into fits of laughter.*) Oh yes, that's the real attraction, God damn it!

ANNA. You're so coarse, that's you all over. Just bear in mind that we'll have a completely different life, different friends – no more chasing hares with that dog-mad judge of yours, and that Zemlyanika creature too. You'll have new friends, the very last word in refinement, counts and such like, people

with a bit of class. To tell you the truth, that's the only thing
that worries me: you come out with the odd word now and
again, the sort you'd never hear in polite society.

MAYOR. So what? Words never harmed anybody.

ANNA. Yes, that's all very well when you were just a mayor.
But this is a completely new life.

MAYOR. It is indeed. D'you know they have two different fish
courses? Whitefish and smelts, it makes your mouth water
just looking at them.

ANNA. Fish – that's all he thinks about ! Well, I want nothing
less than for our house to be the very first in St. Petersburg,
and for my room to be dripping with perfume, so you won't
even need to go in, you'll just stand there with your eyes
closed. (*Closes her eyes and sniffs.*) Mmm, exquisite!

Enter the SHOPKEEPERS.

MAYOR. Aha! And a good day to you, my brave lads!

SHOPKEEPERS. We wish you good health, Your Honour.

MAYOR. So, my fine fellows, how are things? How's business,
eh? Done complaining, have you, you teapot-bashers, you
tweed-stretchers? The arch-fiddlers, the prime chisellers, the
original short weight specialists, complaining about me! Get
much out of it, did you? Oh yes, they'll fling him in jail, you
thought. Well, damn and blast the lot of you, I'll see you in
hell first, you miserable . . .

ANNA. Anton, for heaven's sake – your language!

MAYOR (*Testily*). Oh, the hell with that! Listen, you – that
same Government Inspector, the one you were whingeing to,
is marrying my daughter. You didn't know that, did you, eh?
What've you got to say to that, eh? By God, you're for it
now! Swindling innocent people! A Government contract,
to supply rotten cloth – you skim off a hundred thousand
roubles, and you present me with a measly twenty yards of
the stuff – I'm supposed to give you a medal! By God, if they

get to know about you . . . Oh yes, his gut's sticking out, he must be a shopkeeper, you can't touch him. 'We're as good as any aristocrat,' he says. Yes, well, an aristocrat – yes, I'm talking to you, you pig! – an aristocrat's got to study, and suppose they do whip him at school, at least he'll learn something useful. But what about you? You start out thieving, and your master beats you 'cause you don't know how to swindle right! Ye gods, you're giving short change before you can even say the 'Our Father'! And once you've a big enough paunch on you and you've lined your pockets, my God, the airs and graces of it! You swill down sixteen samovars of tea a day, and think you're the cat's whiskers! Well, I spit in your eye, d'you hear, and your damn pretensions too!

SHOPKEEPERS (*Bowing and scraping*). We're very sorry, Your Honour.

MAYOR. Complain about me, would you? Who was it helped you fiddle the books, when you built that bridge and charged twenty thousand for the wood, when there wasn't even a hundred roubles' worth, eh? It was me, you miserable old goat! Did you forget that? If I point the finger, I could still get you packed off to Siberia. What d'you say to that, eh?

A SHOPKEEPER. Before God, we're truly sorry, Your Honour! It was the devil put us up to it. And we'll never complain again, we promise. We'll do anything you say, only please don't be angry with us!

MAYOR. Don't be angry! Oh yes, you're ready to lick my boots now, and for why? Because I've had a spot of good luck. But if you'd got the upper hand, even slightly, then by God you'd have trampled me into the mud, you swine, and piled logs on top for the hell of it!

SHOPKEEPERS (*Bowing to the ground*). Oh, please, Your Honour, don't ruin us!

MAYOR. Don't ruin you! Oh yes, now it's: 'Don't ruin us!', but what was it before, eh? I tell you, for two pins . . . (*Waves his*

hand dismissively.) Well, let God forgive you. I've said my
piece. I'm not a vindictive man, but you'd better watch your
step from now on. This isn't some upper-class nobody I'm
marrying my daughter to, so congratulations are in order –
you take my meaning? And don't think you can fob me off
with a slice of pickled sturgeon or a sugar-loaf . . . Right,
clear off.

The SHOPKEEPERS *exit. Enter the* JUDGE *and the*
CHARITIES WARDEN.

JUDGE (*still in the doorway*). Can we believe the rumours, Your
Honour? You've had an extraordinary piece of good fortune?

WARDEN. Sir, permit me to offer my congratulations on your
extraordinary good fortune. I was absolutely delighted when
I heard. (*Kisses* ANNA's *hand.*) Anna Andreevna! (*Kisses*
MARYA's *hand.*) Marya Antonovna!

Enter RASTAKOVSKY, *a local dignitary.*

RASTAKOVSKY. Congratulations, Your Honour! May God
grant you and the happy couple long life and abundant
posterity – grandchildren and great-grandchildren! (*Kisses*
ANNA's *hand.*) Anna Andreevna! (*Kisses* MARYA's *hand.*)
Marya Antonovna!

Enter KOROBKIN, *and his* WIFE, *and* LYULYUKOV, *local
dignitaries.*

KOROBKIN. Your Honour, allow me to congratulate you!
Anna Andreevna! (*Kisses* ANNA's *hand.*) Marya Antonovna!
(*Kisses* MARYA's *hand.*)

WIFE. Anna Andreevna, I most sincerely congratulate you on
your good fortune!

LYULYUKOV. Congratulations, Anna Andreevna! (*Kisses*
ANNA's *hand, then turns to the audience, clucks his tongue in mock-
admiration.*) Marya Antonovna! Congratulations! (*Kisses her
hand, then makes the same impudent gesture.*)

Enter numerous VISITORS *in tails and frock-coats, who first kiss* ANNA'*s hand, crying: 'Anna Andreevna!', then* MARYA'*s hand, crying: 'Marya Antonovna!'. Enter* BOBCHINSKY *and* DOBCHINSKY *then, jostling for position.*

BOBCHINSKY. Allow me to offer my congratulations!

DOBCHINSKY. Your Honour, allow me to offer my congratulations!

BOBCHINSKY. On this most propitious occasion!

DOBCHINSKY. Anna Andreevna!

BOBCHINSKY. Anna Andreevna! (*They bend to kiss her hand simultanously and bump their foreheads.*)

DOBCHINSKY. Marya Antonovna! (*Kisses her hand.*) Allow me to congratulate you. You'll be ever so happy, taking the air in a gold dress, and tasting all kinds of dainty dishes. You'll spend your time most agreeably, and . . .

BOBCHINSKY (*interrupting*). Marya Antonovna, allow me to congratulate you! May God grant you prosperity, heaps of roubles, and a teeny little baby boy, this high! (*Demonstrates.*) Yes, so small you can sit him on the palm of your hand! And the little scamp'll cry non-stop: Wah! Wah! Wah!

Enter several more visitors, among them the SUPERINTENDENT OF SCHOOLS *and his* WIFE. *They all kiss the ladies' hands.*

SUPERINTENDENT. Allow me to . . .

HIS WIFE (*rushing ahead*). To offer you my congratulations, Anna Andreevna! (*They kiss.*) I'm absolutely overjoyed. 'Anna Andreevna's daughter's getting married,' they said. 'Good heavens!' I thought, and I was so delighted I said to my husband: 'Just listen to this, Luka my dear – Anna Andreevna's had such a stroke of luck!' 'Well,' I thought, 'Thank God for that!' And I said to him: 'I'm so thrilled for her, I can't wait to tell Anna Andreevna in person!' 'Oh, heavens above,' I thought, 'That's just what Anna Andreevna's been waiting for, a good match for her daughter, and now look what's

happened: she's got exactly what she wanted,' Yes, I was
so overjoyed I couldn't even speak, I just cried and cried,
sobbing my heart out. And Luka says: 'Nastasya my dear,
what are you sobbing for?' 'Oh, dearest Luka,' I says, 'I
don't know myself, the tears just come flooding out.'

MAYOR. Ladies and gentlemen, please be seated! Hey, Mishka,
bring some more chairs in here.

The visitors sit down. Enter the POLICE CHIEF *and the*
CONSTABLES.

POLICE CHIEF. Allow me to congratulate you, Your
Excellency, and wish you many long years of prosperity!

MAYOR. Thank you, thank you! Ladies and gentlemen, please
sit down!

The VISITORS *settle themselves down.*

JUDGE. Now tell us, please, Your Honour, how all this came
about – blow by blow, the whole affair.

MAYOR. Well, it's an extraordinary business: he actually
proposed in person, on the spot.

ANNA. Oh, but so respectfully, and in the most refined
manner. And he put everything so well – quite extraordinary:
'Anna Andreevna,' he says, 'I do this entirely out of respect
for your merits . . . ' Such a handsome, well-educated man,
a man of the most noble principles! 'Believe me, Anna
Andreevna, life isn't worth a kopeck to me, the only thing
I esteem is you, your rare qualities . . . '

MARYA. Mama, for heaven's sake! It was me he said that to!

ANNA. You be quiet – you know nothing about it, it's none
of your business anyway. 'I'm quite overwhelmed, Anna
Andreevna . . . ' Really, the compliments he showered on
me . . . and just when I was going to say: 'We dare not presume to such an honour,' he suddenly went down on his knees,
and said, with the utmost refinement: 'Anna Andreevna,
please don't make me the most wretched of men! Consent
to requite my love, or I shall put an end to my life!'

MARYA. Mama, for pity's sake, it was me he was talking about!

ANNA. Well, of course it was. It was about you too, I'm not denying it.

MAYOR. He had us scared stiff, you know, said he was going to shoot himself. 'I'll shoot myself!', he says, 'I'll shoot myself!'

VISITORS. Heavens above!

JUDGE. Fancy that!

SUPERINTENDENT. It's destiny, that's what it is, the workings of fate.

WARDEN. Fate my foot, sir! It's a just reward for honourable service. (*Aside.*) Trust that swine to have all the the luck!

JUDGE. I dare say I could sell you that pup, Your Honour, the one you were enquiring about.

MAYOR. No, I can't be bothered with pups now.

JUDGE. If you don't want that one, we could agree on another.

KOROBKIN'S WIFE. Oh, Anna Andreevna, you can't imagine how delighted I am at your good fortune!

KOROBKIN. May one ask where our distinguished guest is at present? I heard he'd left town.

MAYOR. Yes, he's gone off for a day on some extremely urgent business.

ANNA. Actually to his uncle, to ask his blessing.

MAYOR. That's right, to ask his blessing. However, tomorrow, without fail . . . (*He sneezes. 'Bless you!' on all sides, merging into a chorus.*) Thank you very much. Anyway, tomorrow without fail . . . (*Sneezes again, another unison chorus, some voices audible above the clamour.*)

POLICE CHIEF. Good health, Your Excellency!

DOBCHINSKY. God grant you a long and happy life!

BOBCHINSKY. A hundred years and pots of money!

WARDEN. Drop dead!

KOROBKIN'S WIFE. Hell mend you!

MAYOR. Thank you kindly, sirs. And I wish you the same.

ANNA. We're planning to move to Petersburg now. I mean, frankly, the air here's so . . . well, it's so provincial. It's quite unpleasant, to be honest. And you see, my husband . . . well, they're going to make him a general.

MAYOR. That's true, sirs. God damn it, I don't half fancy being a general!

SUPERINTENDENT. Pray God they make you one, Your Honour!

RASTAKOVSKY. With God, all things are possible.

JUDGE. Big ships need deep waters.

WARDEN. It's in recognition of your service, sir.

JUDGE (*aside*). That'll be the day, if they ever make him a general! It'd be like sticking a saddle on a cow! No no, my friend, you're not there yet, not by a long shot. There are plenty with cleaner hands than you, and they still haven't made general.

WARDEN (*aside*). Damn the man, who'd believe it – promoting himself to general next! And I wouldn't be surprised if he did it. He's so bumptious the devil himself wouldn't take him! (*Aloud, to the* MAYOR.) You won't forget us now, will you, Your Honour?

JUDGE. I mean, if anything turned up, some sort of business matter needing attention, say, we could still count on your support?

KOROBKIN. I'm taking my boy to Petersburg next year, Your Honour, to put him into the Government service, and I'd be much obliged if you'd use your influence, stand *in loco parentis*, as it were, to the poor little lad.

MAYOR. I shall do everything in my power.

ANNA. Anton dear, you're too ready to make promises. For a start, you won't even have time to think about these things, and in any case, why on earth should you burden yourself with promises?

MAYOR. Well, why not, my dear? I might have the odd spare moment.

ANNA. Yes, I daresay, but you can't go using your influence on behalf of every sort of riff-raff.

KOROBKIN'S WIFE. Did you hear that? Did you hear what she called us?

WOMAN. Oh, she's always been like that. I know her. Sit a pig at table, and she'll show you her trotters!

Enter the POSTMASTER, *out of breath, and clutching a letter with the seal broken.*

POSTMASTER. Oh, sirs! A most extraordinary thing! That fellow we took for a Government Inspector wasn't an Inspector after all!

ALL. What d'you mean – wasn't an inspector?

POSTMASTER. He wasn't an Inspector at all – it says so in this letter.

MAYOR. What? What are you talking about? Says so in what letter?

POSTMASTER. This letter he wrote himself, in his own hand. Somebody brings it in to post, I have a look at the address, I see: 'To Post Office Street'. Well, I was thunderstruck. 'He must've found some irregularity in our postal system,' I think to myself, 'And he's reporting us to the authorities.' So I took it and opened it.

MAYOR. How could you do such a thing!

POSTMASTER. I don't know myself, Your Honour, some supernatural power made me do it. I was just on the point of calling for the courier, to send it off express delivery, but curiosity got the better of me, I swear I've never felt anything like it. 'I can't do it, I can't!' I hear a voice telling me I can't, but something keeps drawing me on! In one ear, I'm hearing: 'Don't dare open that letter, or your goose is cooked!' But in the other ear it's as if some devil's whispering: 'Open it, go on, open it up!' When I pressed down on the sealing-wax, it was as if fire was shooting through my veins, but when I broke it open, honest to God, they were like ice, absolute ice! And my hands were trembling, I nearly passed out.

MAYOR. Good God, man, how dare you open the letter of such an important personage!

POSTMASTER. Well, that's just it, you see – he's not important, and he's not a personage!

MAYOR. So what do you suppose he is, then?

POSTMASTER. Well, he's nothing in particular – God knows what he is.

MAYOR (*incensed*). Nothing in particular! How dare you call him nothing in particular, yes, and God knows what, besides! I'll have you arrested.

POSTMASTER. Who, you?

MAYOR. Yes, me!

POSTMASTER. You can't touch me.

MAYOR. I'll have you know he's marrying my daughter, which'll make *me* a personage, and I'll ship you off to Siberia!

POSTMASTER. Siberia's a long way off, Mister Mayor. You'd better wait till I read this. Well, sirs – shall I read this letter?

ALL. Yes, yes, go on, read it!

POSTMASTER (*reads*). 'My dear Tryapichkin, I write in haste to inform you of the wonders that have befallen me. On the way out here, an infantry captain took me to the cleaners, and the innkeeper was on the point of flinging me in jail, when suddenly the entire town, on account of my Petersburg looks and dress, mistook me for some Governor-General. Anyway, I'm now living off the fat of the the land at the Mayor's house, making desperate advances to his wife and daughter – the only thing being I can't make up my mind which to start with. I think I'll start with the mother first, she looks game for anything. Do you remember when we were down on our luck, trying to fiddle free dinners, and the pastry-cook nearly frogmarched me out, for charging the pies we'd eaten to the King of England's account? Well, it's a different story now. They're all lending me money here, as much as I want. Honestly, you'd die laughing, they're such absolute cretins. I know you write the odd article: you really should put them in your repertoire. The Mayor, for a start, is as thick as two short planks . . . '

MAYOR. That's rubbish! It doesn't say that.

POSTMASTER (*shows him the letter*). Read it yourself!

MAYOR. 'Two short planks . . . ' No, it's not possible. You must've written this.

POSTMASTER. So how could I have written it?

WARDEN. Read on!

SUPERINTENDENT. Yes, read on!

POSTMASTER (*continues*). 'The Mayor is as thick as two short planks . . . '

MAYOR. God damn it, do you need to repeat it! As if we hadn't heard that already.

POSTMASTER (*continues*). Hm . . . hm . . . hm . . . ' . . . two short planks. The Postmaster's a decent chap too . . . ' (*Pauses.*) Well, really! He's been rather rude about me too.

MAYOR. Well, go on, read it out!

POSTMASTER. But what's the point?

MAYOR. Damn it to hell, if you're going to read it, do so! Read the lot!

COMMMISSIONER. Give it here, I'll read it. (*Puts on his spectacles and reads.*) 'The Postmaster's the absolute spit of old Mikheev, our office doorman. I'll bet he's a villain besides, he drinks like a fish.'

POSTMASTER (*to the audience*). Nasty young pup, he needs a good thrashing!

WARDEN (*continues*). 'And as for the Charities Warden, he . . . he . . . he . . .'

KOROBKIN. What've you stopped for?

WARDEN. Actually, the writing's terrible . . . anyway, the man's obviously a scoundrel.

KOROBKIN. Give it to me! My eyes are better than yours. (*Tries to take the letter.*)

WARDEN (*not releasing it*). It's all right, we can skip this bit, it's much clearer further down.

KOROBKIN. Come on, hand it over, I've seen it now.

WARDEN. No no, I'll read it myself. Honestly, the next bit's quite legible.

POSTMASTER. No, read the whole thing! It's all been read out up to now.

ALL. Come on, Artemy, hand it over! (*To* KOROBKIN.) Go on, Korobkin, you read it.

WARDEN. Oh, all right. (*Gives him the letter.*) There you are . . . (*Covers part of it with his finger.*) Read on from here. (*They all crowd round.*)

POSTMASTER. Read it, read it! And no nonsense, mind – read the whole lot!

KOROBKIN (*reads*). 'And as for the Charities Warden, he's a perfect pig in a skull-cap . . .'

WARDEN (*to the audience*). It's not even witty! A pig in a skull-cap! Honestly, who ever heard of a pig in a skull-cap?

KOROBKIN (*continues*). 'And the Schools Superintendent positively reeks of onions . . . '

SUPERINTENDENT (*to the audience*). I swear to God I've never put an onion in my mouth!

JUDGE (*aside*). Well, thank God, at least there's nothing about me!

KOROBKIN (*reads*). 'The Judge . . . '

JUDGE. Damn! (*aloud*). Really, sirs, this letter's far too long. I mean, we don't need to read all this rubbish, do we?

SUPERINTENDENT. Oh yes we do!

POSTMASTER. Read it!

WARDEN. Read the thing!

KOROBKIN (*continues*). 'The Judge, who goes by the name of Lyapkin-Tyapkin, is the absolute last word in *mauvais ton* . . . ' (*Pauses.*) I suppose that's French.

JUDGE. Yes, and God knows what it means! It's bad enough being called a crook, but that's maybe even worse!

KOROBKIN (*continues reading*). 'Anyway, they're a most hospitable and generous lot. Goodbye for now, my dear Tryapichkin. I think I'll follow your lead and take up the pen. It's a bit of a bore, living like this – a fellow needs some sustenance for the soul, after all. You've got to put your mind to higher things, that's how I see it. You can write to me at Podkatilovka, that's in Saratov province . . . ' (*Turns over the letter and reads the address.*) 'To the Honorable Ivan Vasilievich Tryapichkin, third floor right, No. 97 Post Office Street, St Petersburg.'

A LADY. Well, that was completely out of the blue!

MAYOR. He's cut my throat, the swine! I'm dead, I'm finished! I can't see a damn thing, nothing but pigs' snouts – no faces, just pigs' snouts. Get him back here, right now! (*Flapping his arms.*)

POSTMASTER. Fat chance! I told our stationmaster to give him the best team of horses we'd got, made a point of it. Damned if I didn't even give him clearance right through to Saratov.

KOROBKIN'S WIFE. What a mess! What a frightful carry-on!

JUDGE. Yes, well, damn it to hell, sirs – I lent him three hundred roubles!

WARDEN. He's got three hundred roubles of mine too!

POSTMASTER (*sighs*). And mine.

BOBCHINSKY. Plus sixty-five in notes, from Dobchinsky and me, sirs, oh yes.

JUDGE (*spreading his hands helplessly*). Gentlemen, gentlemen, how could this happen? How could we make such idiots of ourselves?

MAYOR (*slapping his forehead*). How could I, you mean? I must be going senile. I've outlived my wits, like some stupid old goat. Thirty years I've been in the service, and not one shopkeeper, not one contractor, could ever get the better of me. Top-flight villains, crooks who could swindle other crooks, I've outsmarted the lot of them, fiddlers and fixers, people who could walk off with the world, I've reeled them all in. Dear God, I've hoodwinked three Governors! Governors, huh! (*Waves his hand in disgust.*) Don't get me started on Governors.

ANNA. But Anton dearest, it's not possible: he's engaged to our Masha . . .

MAYOR (*furious*). Engaged! Engaged my arse! Don't talk to me about engagement! That was just another damn trick, to pull the wool over my eyes. (*In a frenzy.*) Just look at me, eh? Let the whole world, the whole of Christendom, have a good look, see what an ass the Mayor's made of himself! Idiot! Cretin! Stupid old fool! (*Shakes his fist at himself.*) Hey, you! Fat nose! You took that miserable little squirt for a big cheese! Well, he'll be telling it with bells on now, the whole road home! He'll broadcast his story to every corner of the globe. And if that's not bad enough, being made a laughing-stock, some hack, some wretched scribbler'll come along and stick you in a comedy. That's what really hurts! He'll spare nobody, rank and title count for nothing, and they'll all sit grinning and clapping their hands. So what are you laughing at, eh? You're laughing at yourselves, that's what! Oh, you! (*Stamps his foot in rage.*) By God, if I could get my hands on those scribblers! Penpushers! Damn liberals! Devil's spawn! By God, I'd tie the whole lot of you up in a bundle, and grind you to powder! I'd stuff you into the lining of the devil's cap! (*Lashes out with his fist and stamps his heel on the floor. A brief silence then.*) I still can't think straight. I mean, people God wants to punish, he first sends them mad, right? So what was there about this nitwit that remotely resembled a Government Inspector? Not a damn thing! Not so much as the tip of his miserable finger! But suddenly it's all Inspector this, Inspector that! Who first gave out that he was an Inspector, eh? Come on, answer me!

WARDEN (*spreading his arms*). For the life of me, I can't explain how it happened. It was as if some sort of fog came down on us, the devil must've led us astray.

JUDGE. Well, I know who started it! It was those two, they started it, those fine specimens there! (*Points to* DOBCHINSKY *and* BOBCHINSKY.)

BOBCHINSKY. Hold on, hold on! It wasn't me! I never dreamed . . .

DOBCHINSKY. I never said a thing . . .

WARDEN. It was you two all right!

SUPERINTENDENT. Of course it was! You came running in here from the inn like madmen: 'He's here! He's here, and he's not paying his bill!' Oh yes, you found your big cheese all right!

MAYOR. It just had to be you, hadn't it! The town gossips! Damn scandalmongers!

WARDEN. Damn you to hell, both of you, with your Government Inspector and your stupid stories!

MAYOR. You do nothing but snoop around the town, upsetting everybody, you blabbermouths! Dishing the dirt, like a couple of chattering magpies!

JUDGE. Layabouts!

SUPERINTENDENT. Fatheads!

WARDEN. Potbellied runts!

They all start to surround them.

BOBCHINSKY. Oh God, it wasn't me, it was Pyotr Ivanovich!

DOBCHINSKY. No, it wasn't, it was you, Pyotr Ivanovich, you started . . .

BOBCHINSKY. It was not! It was you that started . . .

Enter a GENDARME.

GENDARME. Gentlemen! A Government Inspector, appointed by decree of His Imperial Majesty, has just arrived from St Petersburg, and is staying at the inn, where you are to proceed forthwith.

At these words, they are thunderstruck. Cries of astonishment from the ladies, uttered simultaneously. The whole company then suddenly changes position, and freezes on the spot, as if turned to stone.

Dumb Show

The MAYOR *stands in the centre, like a pillar, with his arms outstretched and his head flung back. To the right are his* WIFE *and* DAUGHTER, *their entire bodies straining towards him; behind them stands the* POSTMASTER, *transformed into a sort of question mark, facing the audience; behind him stands the* SCHOOLS SUPERINTENDENT, *with a look of helpless innocence; behind him, and at the far side of the stage, three visiting ladies, leaning against one another with the most satirical expression on their faces, are looking straight at the* MAYOR'S *family. To the left of the* MAYOR *stands the* CHARITIES WARDEN, *his head cocked to one side as if straining to listen; behind him, the* JUDGE, *with his arms stuck out, is practically squatting on the floor, and moving his lips, as if trying to whistle, or uttter the words: 'Here's another fine mess!' Behind him,* KOROBKIN, *facing the audience, with his eyes screwed up, directs a look of contempt at the* MAYOR; *and behind him again, at the other side of the stage, stand* BOBCHINSKY *and* DOBCHINSKY, *their arms outflung towards each other, openmouthed and goggle-eyed. The other guests stand around like pillars. The petrified company maintain their position for almost a minute and a half. Then the curtain is lowered.*

The end.

Appendix: Pronunciation

Where the stress in English polysyllables mostly falls on the penultimate syllable, Russian stress, which is also heavier, is much less predictable, and this gives rise to pronunciation difficulties, quite apart from its unfamiliar sounds. A particular source of confusion derives from the tendency of Russian vowels to be 'iotated' in speech, i.e., to be preceded by a 'y' sound. English readers of transcriptions incorporating this rule often misconstrue it as an extra syllable, and care should be taken to observe the syllables given below, as well their main accent, which is given in capitals. 'Lyapkin-Tyapkin', for example, consists of four syllables, not six. The Russian names and places transcribed are restricted to those actually spoken, and can only be an approximation.

Abdulin	Ab-DOO-leen
Aleksandrovich	A-lek-SAN-dro-vitch
Andrei, Andreevna	Ahn-DRAY, Ahn-DRAY-yev-na
Anton, Antonovna, Antonovich	An-TOHN, An-TOH-nov-na, An-TOH-no-vitch
Antosha	An-TAW-sha
Artemy	Ar-TEH-mee
Avdotya	Av-DOH-tya
Bobchinsky	Bob-CHIN-ski
Brambeus	Bram-BAY-oos
Cheptovich	Chep-TAW-vitch
Chernyaev	Cher-NYAH-yeff
Derzhimorda	Dyehr-zhee-MAWR-da
Dobchinsky	Dob-CHIN-ski
Fevronya	Fehv-ROH-nyah
Filipp, Filippovich	Fil-LEEP Fil-LEE-po-vitch
Gibner	GIB-ner (hard 'g'.)

Gorokhovaya	Go-ROH-kho-va-ya
Ivan, Ivanov, Ivanovich	Ee-VAHN, Ee-VAH-noff, Ee-VAH-no-vitch
Karamzin	Ka-ram-ZEEN
Khlestakov	Khleh-sta-KOFF
Khlopov	KHLAW-poff
Korobkin	Ko-ROHB-keen
Kostroma	Kaw-stro-MAH
Lyapkin-Tyapkin	LYAP-kin TYAP-kin
Marya	MAR-ya
Miloslavsky	Mee-lo-SLAV-ski
Mikheev	Mee-KHAY-eff (as English 'play'.)
Mishka	MEESH-ka
Nevsky	NYEFF-ski
Nikolai	Nee-koh-LIE (as English 'lie'.)
Osip	OH-sip
Panteleeva	Pan-teh-LAY-yeh-va
Penza	PEN-za
Perepetuya	Peh-reh-peh-TOO-ya
Podkatilovka	Pod-ka-TEE-lof-ka
Poshlyopkina	Po-SHLYOP-kee-na
Prokhorov	PRO-kho-roff
Pugovitsyn	POO-go-vit-seen
Pyotr	PYOTR (one syllable.)
Rastakovsky	Ra-sta-KOFF-ski
Saratov	Sa-RAH-toff
Shchukin	SHCHOO-keen
Shpyokin	SHPYAW-keen
Sidor	SEE-dor
Smirdin	SMEER-deen
Stepan	Styeh-PAN
Svistunov	Svee-stoo-NOFF
Tryapichkin	Tryah-PEECH-kin
Varkhovinsky	Var-kho-VIN-ski
Vasilievich	Va-SEEL-yeh-vitch
Vladimir	Vla-DEE-meer
Yelizaveta	Yeh-lee-zah-VYEH-ta
Yuri	YOO-ri

Zagoskin
Zemlyanika

Zah-GOH-skeen
Zem-lyah-NEE-ka